KENTUCKY, Y'ALL

KENTUCKY,

Y'ALL

A CELEBRATION *of the* PEOPLE *and* CULTURE *of the* BLUEGRASS STATE

BLAIR THOMAS HESS & CAMERON M. LUDWICK

UNIVERSITY PRESS OF KENTUCKY

Published by The University Press of Kentucky

Scholarly publisher for the Commonwealth, serving Bellarmine University, Berea College, Centre College of Kentucky, Eastern Kentucky University, The Filson Historical Society, Georgetown College, Kentucky Historical Society, Kentucky State University, Morehead State University, Murray State University, Northern Kentucky University, Spalding University, Transylvania University, University of Kentucky, University of Louisville, University of Pikeville, and Western Kentucky University.
All rights reserved.

Editorial and Sales Offices: The University Press of Kentucky
663 South Limestone Street, Lexington, Kentucky 40508-4008
www.kentuckypress.com

Illustrations by Jessica Rusher

Library of Congress Cataloging-in-Publication Data

Names: Hess, Blair Thomas, author. | Ludwick, Cameron M., author.
Title: Kentucky, y'all : a celebration of the people and culture of the Bluegrass State / Blair Thomas Hess & Cameron M. Ludwick.
Other titles: Kentucky, you all
Description: Lexington, Kentucky : University Press of Kentucky, [2024] | Includes bibliographical references and index.
Identifiers: LCCN 2024010596 | ISBN 9781985900721 (hardcover) | ISBN 9781985900738 (paperback) | ISBN 9781985900752 (pdf) | ISBN 9781985900745 (epub)
Subjects: LCSH: Kentucky—Social life and customs. | Kentucky—Miscellanea.
Classification: LCC F456.2 .H47 2024 | DDC 976.9—dc23/eng/20240313
LC record available at https://lccn.loc.gov/2024010596

Member of the Association
of University Presses

To all who are proud of where they come from—
the people, the place, the history—no matter
where that happens to be. We sure are.

CONTENTS

INTRODUCTION

Heaven must be a Kentucky kind of place.

DANIEL BOONE

Once, we met a husband and wife in the parking lot of a small-town Kentucky hardware store. As we helped them load up their truck, they shared that they were new to the area and had just bought a farm with a little three-bedroom house in Shelby County, sight unseen. They were relocating from a big city in New England and were looking forward to the quiet life and the warm community that one often finds in small towns in more southern states. Their new home was just a few miles down the road from a young couple they met who had done nearly the same—relocated from out West because they wanted a welcoming place to raise a family where they'd know their neighbors. By the time we parted ways in that parking lot, we'd gifted them a Kentucky travel book (written by us, of course), a list of some of our favorite local restaurants and weekend stops, and a bottle of bourbon that we just happened to have on us for an occasion such as this one.

"Who are you all?" the man asked us. "The Official Kentucky Welcoming Committee?"

We just might be. We pride ourselves on welcoming others to our home state, and we invite everyone to experience the adventures, kindness, and community like a fellow Kentuckian.

At the state's most eastern point, deep in the foothills of the Appalachian Mountains, it would be difficult to draw a perfect dividing line separating Kentucky from its neighbors. But if you step over that invisible line, Kentucky's tall oak trees and meandering creeks—while similar in appearance to their counterparts in the Virginias—all but close in and quietly encourage you to journey westward. Steep mountains and dense forest of the east blend into rolling hills of Bluegrass. The roads of central Kentucky are framed by black wooden fences, and grand horse barns dot the horizon. The north has its river towns, the south, its rugged gorges. Through cave country and even further west—the flatlands where row crops thrive—you'll realize that Kentucky is as richly diverse as it is lovely.

Writer Jesse Stuart called Kentucky America's heart. Pioneer Daniel Boone called it Heaven. Kentuckians, born here or transplanted, living here or moved away, simply call the state home.

Kentucky's complicated history gives it a unique place among the fifty states. It straddled the divide during the Civil War, claims Abe Lincoln as its own (against the pretensions of another, unnamed, state to the north), and is unsure whether to declare itself southern or midwestern. And Kentuckians, quite aware of the stereotypes, would like to set the record straight: we do own shoes (even if we aren't always wearing them), and our charming drawl does not mean that we're slow-witted—our thinkers, writers, scientists, musicians, and artists can stand up against those of any state. After all, writers Hunter S. Thompson, Robert Penn Warren, Barbara Kingsolver, Wendell Berry, bell hooks, Jesse Stuart, and Bobbie Ann Mason are all Kentuckians. So are journalists Diane Sawyer, Alice Dunnigan, Helen Thomas, and Nick Clooney (not to mention his famous sister Rosemary Clooney and his son, George). John T. Thompson, inventor of the Thompson submachine gun (better known as the Tommy gun) was born in Newport. Nobel Prize winner Phillip Allen Sharp, who co-discovered RNA splicing and considerably advanced research on cancer and hereditary diseases, was born in Falmouth. Garrett Morgan of Paris, Kentucky, invented the first respiratory protective hood, which led to the modern gas mask, and also went on to invent the first automatic, tricolor traffic signal. We could brag about Kentucky all day—and often, we do.

We've been friends since forever and share a passion for travel; we love to get out into the world and meet new people. Several years ago, we decided to begin our explorations in our own backyard and started with the places that everyone has heard about—Mammoth Cave, a national park and the world's longest cave system, and Cumberland Falls, fondly known as the Niagara of the South. But soon we found ourselves at the Monroe County Marble Club Super Dome, playing a rousing game of Rolley Hole in the dirt. We were eating mutton barbecue sandwiches while petting the mayor of Rabbit Hash—a dog—and clutching hands as we walked through a haunted tuberculosis hospital on the outskirts of Louisville after midnight.

Over the years, our travels—and the four travel guides we wrote together—have taken us to food festivals and famous bourbon distilleries, to airports and cemeteries and race tracks and historic monuments. And along the parkways and the backroads, as we met our fellow Kentuckians, we learned things about our neighbors and their communities that we couldn't learn from reading historical markers or maps or history books. We hit the road to see Kentucky, but it didn't take us long to realize that we were really meeting Kentucky for the first time.

We grew up near each other in the central part of the state, in multigenerational Kentucky families with annual Kentucky traditions. With family ties in the metropolitan areas of Louisville, the northern counties around Maysville, and the far western corner near Lake Barkley, we felt like we had a pretty good idea of what Kentucky was all about. From a young age we could rattle off college basketball starting lineups and recite the odds and trainers of favorite Derby contenders. When we were teething babies, our parents rubbed bourbon on our gums. We rode horses and helped our grandmothers fry chicken and could write you a book report about the great Honest Abe. But we came to understand that ours was just one version of this fascinating state made up of people from many backgrounds and cultures, people who celebrate their own traditions and who hold differing principles and beliefs.

We've always loved a quote from Edith Wharton (not a Kentuckian, but we can forgive the great American novelist that single fault), "One of the great things about travel is that you find out how many good, kind people there are." We have found Wharton's observation to be true. Through our combined travels to nearly all fifty states and many other countries, we've found that nowhere is it truer than in Kentucky—citizens across the Commonwealth welcomed us into their homes and their communities.

On the interstates and backroads, from the eastern mountains to the most western tippity tip, we've basked in the state's beauty and spent time at its most boastful tourist destinations, soaking in all of the available history. We've slept in wigwams (Wigwam Village No. 2 in Cave City), discovered Kentucky's own Stonehenge (in Munfordville), walked alongside buffalo (a must-see stop in western Kentucky's Land Between the Lakes), and attended more battle reenactments than would seem possible (the Battle of Perryville every October is probably our favorite). And, perhaps most importantly, we have spent hours, weeks, years talking with our fellow Kentuckians—young and old, born here and naturalized. These travels and conversations all confirm that Kentucky is more than bourbon, fried chicken, and race horses. Kentucky is home, a place of tradition and a place where new traditions are constantly being created.

Albert B. Chandler, more fondly known in these parts as Happy, represented Kentucky in the US Senate and served as the state's forty-fourth and forty-ninth governor. He was a native of Corydon in Henderson County (current population 720) and once said, "I never met a Kentuckian who wasn't either thinking about going home or actually going home." Every Kentuckian we've met has some sort of emotional tether to this place. Hard to put your finger on, this melancholy longing, or wistfulness, or yearning may summon visions of four-plank fences and porch swings, or mountains and hollers, or endless fields of row crops. Maybe it's just the desire to be with people you love in the place that you love.

It's one reason two friends set out on this journey together many years ago. Two of Kentucky's proudest advocates, we want to help others discover our state's hidden history, its stories, destinations, and culture—even the strange parts. Why do we wear big hats to horse races? Why do we make our whiskey with corn? Why do we pronounce Versailles, "Ver-sales"? Why does a blanket of roses receive an annual police escort, and what exactly is burgoo? And more than that, what has growing up in Kentucky taught us about traditions and community? What makes the state confusing, yet so hard to leave?

In this book, we've compiled favorite Kentucky oddities, cultural quirks, customs, and rites of passage, some internalized in our youth and some discovered as we traveled and met the people of the Commonwealth. Kentucky readers may find familiarity and perhaps some comfort in these collective stories and memories. And we are excited to share all this with those who may just be saddling up.

As friends and as Kentuckians, we've enjoyed every minute of traveling and learning about the Bluegrass State together. We're grateful for the people we've met who have shared their perspectives on the history, culture, and traditions of this state. They've made our version of Kentucky broader. We hope that you will learn to better understand and appreciate Kentucky or perhaps fall in love with it all over again.

We're proud to be a part of Kentucky's story, no matter how big or small that part may be. And we're with Jesse Stuart on this one—Kentucky is the heart of this country. Welcome home.

PART 1
BIGGER THAN FRIED CHICKEN

When we're gathered around tables with our family and friends in Kentucky, there's never a shortage of good food or great company. And aren't some of the very best memories built around food? Our grandmother's beaten biscuits every Christmas Eve, an early dinner at a favorite restaurant on the Kentucky River to stock up on beer cheese, or a warm bowlful of burgoo on a chillier-than-average race day—these are the flavors and experiences that put the "homey" in My Old Kentucky Home.

Kentucky is home to the inventors of Bibb lettuce, the cheeseburger, burgoo, Hot Browns, and beer cheese, just to name a few. True, in some cases, others have tried to claim credit for these culinary masterpieces (we're looking at you, Humpty Dumpty Drive-In in Denver, Colorado, over there trying to call dibs on the cheeseburger). But there are some dishes that are just true Kentucky staples and we'll tell you why.

We know how to make (and eat) good food, and we've been doing it like our grandparents and their grandparents before them for generations. Some of our dishes may strike the outsider as curious. After all, Kentuckians like to eat our bread with a spoon (go ahead, give spoonbread a try) and Western Kentucky lays claim to the World's Largest Country Ham and Biscuit (at its 1985 debut at the Trigg County Country Ham Festival, the enormous biscuit weighed four thousand pounds).

Some of the most mouth-watering dishes had a beginning born of necessity. Much of Kentucky's culinary history is rooted in the cultures of the earliest settlers, who used the resources at hand for their survival. Today, we age our ham in salt because we like the taste, but traditionally it was a way to get the meat to last longer. Similarly, our German ancestors in northern Kentucky taught us to add oats to our sausage to stretch a meal; our forefathers made a delicious stew from whatever they could hunt; and a hotel chef stacked together the limited ingredients in his kitchen to create a now-famous open-faced sandwich.

So, grab your plate and join us, y'all. This meal has multiple courses and great stories to chew on.

1 | CURIOUS CULINARY PAIRINGS

We suppose it depends on your definition of curious—we've seen college kids and pregnant women eat way weirder combinations of things—but there have certainly been accusations of stranger-than-usual food pairings in traditional Kentucky dishes. Our favorite chefs, backyard grill masters, grandmothers, and other culinary masterminds regularly combine ingredients that haven't traditionally been seen as, well, related.

The Best Beer and Cheese Pairing

A famous instance of these less-than-typical pairings is beer cheese, which originated on the banks of the Kentucky River in the 1940s. It may seem commonplace today, but when Johnnie Allman first served a spicy version of this sharp cheese delicacy at the Driftwood Inn in Winchester, it was a combo many had never tasted. A native of Richmond, Allman was a newspaper reporter and a police officer before he opened his first restaurant on the river near Boonesborough. It was there that he whipped up his now-famous Snappy Cheese, a recipe he perfected with his cousin Joe, a head chef at a racetrack in Phoenix, Arizona. That southwestern influence could explain why Snappy Cheese, and the many imitators that have followed, tends to be spicy.

The trick is to start with a sharp cheddar cheese, add enough beer to provide flavor and texture, and then not tell anyone what secret spices were added to give it that quintessential punch. At least, that's how the very best beer cheese makers do it. But we'll give you artisans a head start: many spice combinations use garlic, dry mustard, horseradish, and cayenne pepper. Some are mild, many are hot, and all are delicious.

We've already been asked: will any old beer work? The answer: sort of. Any beer can be used in beer cheese, but the great makers will advise using one you like. Beer gives beer cheese its distinctive flavor, so make it one of your favorites. Lagers tend to work best because they are smooth and flavorful but don't overpower the other ingredients. A pro tip: Flat beer is always best, so let it sit out on the countertop for a day first. Beer cheese is typically served with crackers and raw vegetables, but we've seen it dressed up with fancy sausages and other charcuterie delights. We say, you do you.

Now that we've related the real origins of beer cheese, we can tell a few of the contradicting stories as well. Many believe it originated in bars in the late nineteenth century as a way to use the flat, unsellable beer. Perhaps. It's also similar to Obatzter, a cheese spread that originated in Bavaria, made from soft cheese, butter, spices, and beer. However, Kentuckians know the truth: Mr. Allman mixed up what we know as beer cheese at that small diner in Clark County. In 2013, the Kentucky Legislature decreed the county to be its birthplace, and that makes it official. Winchester hosts a Beer Cheese Festival each summer—always on the hottest weekend in June.

A Classic Kentucky Beer Cheese

2 10-ounce pieces of extra sharp cheddar cheese
2 cloves garlic
7 ounces beer (of your choice)
⅛ teaspoon salt
Hot sauce to taste

Grate cheese and garlic in a food processor; add the remaining ingredients and mix until thoroughly blended. The mixture—which makes about three cups—will be soft but will harden in the refrigerator. Serve with crackers, celery sticks, radish roses, and pretzels.

A Few Oats Will Go a Long Way

Northern Kentucky has a history rich with unique traditions and fare, brought by German settlers who emigrated to the area along the Ohio River in the eighteenth century. One of the most delicious traditional dishes is goetta, a meat and grain sausage. Its pronunciation is a little tricky. Kentuckians say "ged-da" or "get-uh," but our German ancestors more likely pronounced it "gutta."

Goetta is made up of ground meat (usually pork or a combination of pork and beef), steel-cut oats, onion, and a collection of spices. It was traditionally a peasant dish, and the oats were added not for the taste but to stretch out servings of meat over several meals. Today, we consider it a treat.

Here's how to prepare it: Slice the goetta sausage into half-inch patties, similar to traditional breakfast sausage, or crumble it up and brown it like a hash in a skillet over medium heat. Bon appétit, y'all!

Which Meat Do I Add to Burgoo?

Burgoo is to Kentucky what gumbo is to Louisiana or clam chowder is to New England. This historic dish can be traced back to the early days of the state, but few can agree about the who, when, where, or why of it. It may have come from bulgur porridge, which was a staple of sailors back in the 1700s. It's equally possible that the word "burgoo" is a mashup of the words "barbecue" and "ragout," two filling and frugal dishes popular with early settlers of the Bluegrass State.

One of our favorite versions of the story goes like this. In the 1860s, French chef Gustave Jaubert worked for Confederate general John Hunt Morgan, who resided in Lexington. He served the general "bird stew," and the name, said in a French accent, was misheard as "burgoo." The chef was later hired by Buffalo Trace Distillery in Frankfort to cook large iron kettles of his filling stews for its employees.

Regardless of its origins, burgoo is a sort of catch-all hunter's stew with recipes that vary as widely as the dish's ingredients. No two chefs make it the same way, and the recipes are often kept secret. Jaubert's reportedly included beef, chicken, rabbit, tomatoes, corn, potatoes, and onions. Some versions are a little bit wilder, and, depending on the hunting season, may include venison, squirrel, or game birds.

Some of the best burgoos are made over a fire and stirred non-stop. Families still sit around the campfire, or in the kitchen, cooking big pots of stew so thick the spoon stands up in it and adding the ingredients they just happen to have. We've had burgoo made with a variety of meats including, but not limited to, beef, pork, chicken, mutton, and rabbit, along with tomatoes, corn, potatoes, onions, lima beans, and okra.

Burgoo is a staple at family and church picnics, political rallies, and racetracks across the Commonwealth—even the 1932 Kentucky Derby winner was named Burgoo King. One of our favorite versions of this comfort dish comes served in a small Styrofoam™ bowl at Keeneland Race Track in Lexington.

Copycat Keeneland Burgoo

1 cup diced celery

1 cup diced carrot

1 cup diced onion

3 pounds stew meat

12-ounce can tomato puree

2 pounds fresh okra, sliced

1 tablespoon beef base

1 teaspoon Worcestershire sauce

1 cup sherry wine

3 pounds diced potatoes

1 teaspoon ground thyme

1 teaspoon dry sage

1 teaspoon garlic powder

1 teaspoon dry oregano
Water (as needed)
Cornstarch (if desired)

Brown stew meat with herbs. Add remaining ingredients and
cover with water. Bring to a boil, and reduce to simmer for a
minimum of three hours, stirring occasionally. Before serving,
combine water and cornstarch and add the mixture slowly,
stirring until the burgoo reaches the desired thickness. Serves
ten to twelve.

Kentuckians Will Put Bourbon in Anything

Any true Kentuckian will tell you that we drink our bourbon neat—
but we're willing to eat it as well. We love our bourbon, and we
love our food, so the prospect of combining the two is delightful.

Rebecca Ruth Candy makes a variety of delicious treats, but it
is most famous for creating the distinctively Kentucky bourbon
ball. These bite-sized confections incorporate bourbon and dark
chocolate and are each topped with a pecan. Ruth Hanly originally
got the idea for mixing up a sugary bourbon filling at Frankfort's
sesquicentennial celebration in 1936. She worked for two years to
perfect the still-secret process.

Ruth Hanly and her friend Rebecca Gooch, both substitute
schoolteachers, founded Rebecca Ruth Candy in Frankfort in
1919. After making chocolates for friends and family each holiday
season, the two did something unusual for women in the early
twentieth century. Rebecca and Ruth rented the barroom at the
Frankfort Hotel, which had closed due to Prohibition, and went
into business. Today, the candy company is run by Ruth's son,
John, and his son, Charles, and their bourbon balls are available
across the country.

Although bourbon balls may be the most famous sweets in
the Commonwealth, they aren't the only candy invented in Kentucky. Airheads were first developed by Steve Bruner in Erlanger,

Kentucky, in 1985 and are still made here today. There are a variety of other Kentucky candies for your sweet tooth, like caramel marshmallow Modjeskas (pronounced "mo-jess-kahs"), cream pull candy, or a Blue Monday bar (because everyone needs something a little sweet to get them through a blue Monday).

2 | KENTUCKY KITCHEN TRADITIONS

At a Kentucky county fair (some informal rule requires these to be held only on the absolute hottest days of summer), it's a good idea to grab a deep-fried Twinkie and head to the 4-H tent to see all of the prize-winning treasures. Among the blue-ribbon tapestries and quilts, you'll happen upon the largest pumpkin, the prettiest tomato, the most delicious transparent pie, or the show-stopping country ham—you're in for a real treat.

These are the creations of talented artisans who have been perfecting their recipes, their processes, and their craft their whole lives. Kentuckians know how to keep a secret recipe close to the vest and how to pass age-old traditions down to the next generation.

Our food is unique and diverse, and our culinary inventions originate from the variety of backgrounds of the earliest settlers of the Bluegrass State. Kentucky's notable chefs and its run-of-the-mill family cooks alike have contributed to the state's food traditions and innovations, which include Bibb lettuce, cheeseburgers, and chewing gum.

John B. Bibb of Frankfort, a lawyer and amateur horticulturist, developed a variety of butterhead lettuce in the 1860s in his backyard greenhouse. Now known as Bibb lettuce, this limestone lettuce is available in grocery stores and restaurants across the country. In 1934, restaurateur Carl Kaelin was the first to put a piece of American cheese on a beef patty at his restaurant; he promptly finished three in one sitting and found that he had invented the cheeseburger. In 1860, Kentucky drugstore owner John Colgan used his store's extra chicle and changed how chewing gum was made. Chicle, a milky substance found in sapodilla trees, was often used as an ingredient in cough syrup. Colgan mixed it with balsam tolu extract and powdered sugar, creating a delicious, chewy substance that was a major improvement on old chewing gums, which were typically flavorless pieces of wax.

Impressed yet? There are so many well-kept secrets in kitchens across the state.

Curing a Country Ham

A country ham is not the city pig's processed country cousin, nor is it confined to dinner tables outside of metropolitan areas. Country ham is the common name for the dry-cured hind leg of a (city or country) pig, and it is a staple of Kentucky meals. The process of curing a country ham, which started out of necessity, has been perfected over the years in the Bluegrass State.

A dry-cured ham is rubbed with salt and seasonings, smoked, and then aged anywhere from four months to three years. It's a process as old as the state, brought over by British colonists who had learned to preserve meat for long journeys—like crossing the Atlantic Ocean. Most often the hams are placed in salt boxes for about a month, dry rubbed with pepper, and then hung from ceiling hooks and smoked at a low temperature, using hickory wood, for up to five weeks. If hams are hung during the hot months, the high temperatures will sweat out the moisture. Then the aging process—which often lasts about a year but can stretch to several—begins.

In Princeton, a Caldwell County town in the western part of the state, Colonel Bill Newsom's Aged Kentucky Country Ham has been curing pork hind legs the same way since the 1600s—packed in salt in the coldest months of the year, smoked over nineteenth-century iron kettles, and released at the end of each summer. At Broadbent's in Kuttawa, they won't divulge how they cure their famous country ham, but they've been doing it deliciously since 1909.

The result is salty and chewy and, if eaten by a Kentuckian, served on a biscuit. Sure, we've seen it fancied up in trendy restaurants alongside fruits and cheeses or skillet fried at the roadside diner in redeye gravy. But we prefer ours on a buttermilk biscuit, and in Kentucky, you might just happen upon the World's Largest Country Ham and Biscuit.

The official Guinness World Record biscuit first debuted at the Trigg County Country Ham Festival in 1985. It weighed four thousand pounds. Over fifteen thousand people were there to view the biscuit, and a parade was held in its honor. Since then, the recipe has been halved. Each October, a mere two-thousand-pound biscuit, measuring 10½ feet in diameter, is baked in a custom-built oven and removed by forklift during the festival. The recipe includes 150 pounds of flour, 2 pounds of salt, 6½ pounds of sugar, 39 pounds of shortening, 39 cups of water, and 13 gallons of buttermilk. Sixteen large baked country hams are added before it is served.

However epic, that country ham isn't the most expensive. That distinction belongs to a $10-million ham. No, we aren't kidding, and no, there isn't anything particularly different or special about this country ham. Showcased each year at the Kentucky Farm Bureau's annual Ham Breakfast at the Kentucky State Fair is a country ham that costs more than a Rolls Royce. The tradition began in 1964 as a way to promote the pork industry; interested bidders could buy a ticket at the door and win the ham for a couple hundred dollars (that very first ham was auctioned for $124). Today, attendance at the August event has grown to more than two thousand guests, and the auction price of the country ham has also increased. In 2014, it went for $2 million; in 2023, the ham—an eighteen pounder from Broadbent B&B Foods—was won at a whopping $10 million. Proceeds from the auction are donated to a charity of the winning bidder's choosing. That ham must be awfully difficult to slice.

Kentucky's Fairest Fare

Outside of food festivals, there is no better place to get a sampling of the state's most authentic fare than at the . . . *fair.* Each August, Kentuckians flock to the state fairgrounds in Louisville for a week of games, carnival rides, livestock competitions, horse shows, and some of the best—or at least some of the most unusual—food that the state has to offer. While the customary fair staples, such as funnel cakes, corn dogs, and smoked turkey legs, are always a good choice, Kentucky likes to put its own spin on things.

For the deep-fried May Day pie, a Kentucky take on deep-fried Oreos and Twinkies, one of the state's most famous desserts is popped into some hot oil to make it even more delicious. Visitors can also taste butt fries, which consist of smoked pork or mutton butt, cheddar cheese sauce, red onions, jalapeño peppers, and barbecue sauce on top of fries. Or there's the sweet and salty option of a donut cheeseburger—a delicious Carl Kaelin favorite topped with lettuce, tomato, and mayo layered between two glazed donuts.

And that's not even the strangest combination. A few years ago, in an effort to bring back more local meat to the Kentucky State Fair, local entrepreneurs put together a partnership with state cattle farmers, the Kentucky Cattlemen's Association, and Kentucky's newly revitalized hemp industry to serve up a new state fair favorite: the hemp hot dog.

Once an important crop in Kentucky, hemp has been making a comeback in recent years. Because it's closely related to marijuana, hemp sometimes gets a bad rap. But the plant has a lot of potential uses, not least of which is in a good all-beef hot dog. These locally sourced and processed beef and pork hot dogs are cooked with hemp oil and a sprinkling of crushed hemp hearts to add a roasted nut flavor to the quarter-pound bratwurst. There's nothing dodgy about this tasty treat—the US Department of Agriculture permits the use of hemp oil and seeds as ingredients for flavoring meat, and hemp doesn't contain enough tetrahydrocannabinol (better known as THC) to induce a high.

Fry Chicken Like the Colonel

"Hey Siri, how do you fry chicken?" No judgment here—who hasn't wished for a little assistance as they stood in the kitchen, hands covered in a buttermilk and flour paste, and danced in front of the stovetop trying to escape the oil popping out of the cast iron skillet? We're not saying we've been there, we're just saying we see you.

Fried chicken, once a luxury because it was difficult for families to find and afford a tender spring chicken, is now a Kentucky staple fit for all occasions. After all, it was basically reinvented and perfected in the Bluegrass State by the one and only Colonel.

Colonel Harland Sanders is best known for his eleven-herbs-and-spices fried chicken and the fast food chain he founded: Kentucky Fried Chicken (known today as KFC). Sanders was born in Henryville, Indiana, in 1890, but it was in Kentucky that he invented his famous recipe for chicken and built his delicious empire. Sanders got his start in the kitchen at a young age. His father died when he was five, and Sanders took care of and cooked for his younger brother and sister while his mother was working. He dropped out of school in the seventh grade, but he was a hard worker and held many jobs—farmer, streetcar conductor, railroad fireman, and insurance salesman. At forty, he was running a service station in Kentucky, where he cooked to feed hungry travelers. His food was so popular that he moved his operation to a restaurant across the street and began perfecting his fried chicken recipe.

In 1952, Sanders closed that restaurant and focused on franchising his chicken business. By 1964, he had more than six hundred franchised outlets and sold his interest in the company for $2 million. Folks with memories of it tell how the Colonel, after having sold his shares, would walk into various franchises and criticize the recipes and methods. And he would jump back on the line to make sure folks knew how it was done! As it grew, the corporation had to modify the Colonel's "complicated" original recipe. Today, KFC Corporation is still based in Louisville, and seventeen thousand restaurants in more than 115 countries and territories around the world serve finger lickin' good chicken to more than 12 million customers each day.

The Colonel died in 1980 at ninety years old, still rocking his Van Dyke beard, string bow tie, and white suit. But his fried chicken legacy lives on. Here are directions to try his version at home:

Chicken: A whole chicken's worth of pieces: at least two breasts, two thighs, two drumsticks, and two wings.

Spices: Paprika, onion salt, chili powder, black pepper, celery salt, dried sage, garlic powder, allspice, dried oregano, dried basil, and dried marjoram. (His taste testing team must have had fun!)

Batter: An egg white, all-purpose flour, brown sugar, kosher salt.

The tools: One does not attempt to fry chicken without a good amount of vegetable oil and a trusty cast iron skillet. An indestructible combination of iron and carbon, a cast iron skillet holds heat well and distributes it evenly. Older than America, cast-iron cookware was brought to the states by the colonists. Even an old cast iron skillet covered in rust can be easily brought back to life, and if treated properly, it'll outlive any other skillet in the kitchen.

Fry it up like the Colonel: preheat the skillet and oil; mix the spices, flour, and brown sugar. Dip chicken pieces in egg white to lightly coat them, and then transfer to flour mixture. Turn a few times and make sure the flour mix is really stuck to the chicken. Repeat with all the chicken pieces, and then let them rest for five minutes so the crust can dry a bit. Fry chicken in batches. Breasts and wings should take twelve to fourteen minutes, and legs and thighs will need a few more minutes. Chicken pieces are done when a meat thermometer inserted into the thickest part reads 165 degrees F. Let chicken drain on a few paper towels when it comes out of the fryer. Serve hot.

What Is a Kentucky Colonel?

So, what's in a name? While Sanders held many jobs in his life, he never enlisted in the military. Governor Ruby Lafoon named Sanders a Kentucky Colonel, the highest title of honor bestowed by the governor of Kentucky, to mark the success of Kentucky Fried Chicken. Harland Sanders became Colonel Sanders, which he is still called today.

While the modern version of this state honor is not a military rank or title, it does have its origins in the armed forces. The title of Kentucky Colonel dates back to around 1813. After a highly successful campaign during the War of 1812, the Kentucky Militia disbanded, and Governor Isaac Shelby commissioned Charles S. Todd, an officer in the campaign, as an aide on his staff. At the time, Todd's official rank was colonel. For a few years, this aide-de-camp role was occupied by individuals who had served in the military. But the position took on a more ceremonial function in the late 1800s.

By the late 1920s, the Colonels formed a society, which had its first formal meeting in 1931 in Frankfort. It became a nonpolitical brotherhood that aimed to advance Kentucky and Kentuckians. Today, Colonel is an honorary title bestowed upon individuals who work to promote and serve the state.

3 | RECIPES THAT WIN, PLACE, AND SHOW

Since the Kentucky Derby's first race in 1875, this annual experience has had a monumental impact, not just on horse racing but equally on the state's culture and food. The Derby is not simply those two minutes—deemed the fastest in sports—when the horses are running. It's the pageantry of the day, the big hats, the constant chatter about the morning line, the changing odds, and the purse. It's the horses at the beginning of their careers—three-year-olds (mostly males, but fillies can also run) with funny names like Seattle Slew, War Admiral, Gallant Fox, and American Pharoah. It's the singing of "My Old Kentucky Home" as the horses march down the track toward the starting gate.

Kentuckians' emotional tether to the Bluegrass is never stronger than on the first Saturday in May. On Derby Day, as people across the world turn their eyes on the Bluegrass State, we get to show off our great traditions, and we're never more proud to call Kentucky home.

Along with the horses, steeples, a blanket of roses—which receives a police escort to Churchill Downs ahead of the Derby each year—and mint juleps, Derby Day brings its share of culinary treats as well. Take the always popular Hot Brown. The Brown Hotel serves about eight hundred of these open-faced sandwiches each week, but closer to Derby Day, that number increases to nearly four hundred a day. Derby pie? Well, the Kern family in Louisville, inventors of the delicious trademarked Derby-Pie®, sell more than one hundred thousand of these desserts each year.

A proper Kentucky Derby celebration requires a respectable menu. Here are a few famous dishes that will be in the money!

Part three of this book gives more information about the origins of the Derby and how to dress for the event. Part four offers even more recipes and party tips.

Win: How to Stack a Hot Brown

The oft-uttered, and rarely accurate, phrase "We have absolutely nothing to eat!" has sometimes led to the throwing together of the best meals. The Hot Brown was created late one Friday night when a hotel with a ballroom full of hungry—and slightly intoxicated—dancers, was faced with this very predicament. The kitchen was low on supplies, but telling the crowd it had nothing to serve them was just not an option.

The story may begin with Madeleine Astor. She was famous as the wife of John Jacob Astor, an American business tycoon and one of the country's wealthiest men during the Gilded Age. She was also famous as a survivor of the RMS *Titanic* (her husband did not survive). Also a famous hostess, Astor used to serve her party guests toast with melted cheese and eggs in between dances. Perhaps Chef Fred K. Schmidt had her tradition top-of-mind when he invented the Brown Hotel's famous Hot Brown.

In the 1920s, the popular downtown Louisville hotel drew more than twelve hundred guests each evening, and more on the weekends, for its dinner dance. After a night of dancing, having worked up quite the appetite, the guests would make their way into the hotel's restaurant for a bite to eat. One particularly busy night, Chef Schmidt was out of just about everything in his kitchen. Desperately looking for ingredients to feed a room full of hungry and tired dancers, he pulled out all of the meats that he had, but he didn't have enough of any of them to feed everyone. In a moment of inspiration, he began stacking bread, turkey, bacon, and a rich cheese sauce and placing the combination under the broiler.

This open-faced turkey and bacon sandwich with a delicate Mornay sauce became a Kentucky tradition. The Brown Hotel still uses Schmidt's original recipe: heavy cream and pecorino Romano cheese for the Mornay, sliced roasted turkey breast, Texas toast, crispy bacon slices, Roma tomatoes, paprika, and parsley.

The Legendary Brown Hotel Hot Brown
(makes two Hot Browns)

1½ tablespoons salted butter
1½ tablespoons all-purpose flour
1½ cups heavy cream
¼ cup pecorino Romano cheese, plus extra for garnish
Pinch of ground nutmeg
Salt and pepper
14 ounces sliced roasted turkey breast, sliced thick
4 slices Texas toast (crusts trimmed)
4 slices bacon
1 Roma tomato, sliced lengthwise
Paprika
Parsley

In a two-quart saucepan, melt butter and slowly whisk in flour until combined to form a thick paste or roux. Continue to cook the roux for two minutes over medium-low heat, stirring frequently. Whisk heavy cream into the roux and cook over medium heat until the cream begins to simmer, about two to three minutes. Remove sauce from heat and slowly whisk in pecorino Romano cheese until the Mornay sauce is smooth. Add nutmeg, salt, and pepper to taste.

For each Hot Brown, place one slice of toast in an oven-safe dish and cover with seven ounces of turkey. Cut the remaining pieces of toast in half diagonally and lean two toast points against the base of the sandwich. Then take two slices of Roma tomato and stack on top of the turkey. Pour half of the sauce over each dish, completely covering it. Sprinkle with additional cheese. Place the entire dish under a broiler until the cheese begins to brown and bubble. Remove and cross two pieces of crispy bacon on top. Sprinkle the whole thing with paprika, parsley, and a bit more cheese, and serve immediately.

Place: What's in the Perfect May Day Pie?

Nothing complements a tasty mint julep quite like a slice of May Day pie. Gooey and chocolatey, made better with pecans or walnuts, and, according to taste, a splash (or ten) of bourbon. May Day pie is welcome year-round, but it is never more enjoyed than during Derby season.

The official Derby-Pie® was invented more than fifty years ago as the specialty pastry of the Melrose Inn in Prospect, Kentucky, just outside of Louisville. George Kern, manager of the restaurant, developed the Derby-Pie® with the help of his parents. The family closed the Melrose Inn in the 1960s but kept the pie business, and today they operate a commercial kitchen in Louisville where they still bake and ship their famous dessert.

It is worth noting that pecans and walnuts, while delicious, have historically been (and really, still are) a bit expensive. Many families can't spare the extra cash for such a treat, but Kentucky has a delicious pie that is very economical. The transparent pie made its first appearance in a Kentucky newspaper advertisement in the 1890s. It's sort of like Indiana's sugar pie, New England's chess pie, or Pennsylvania's shoofly pie—a super sweet, gooey pie made from sugar, eggs, and milk.

Transparent pie was popularized by Magee's Bakery, which started in Maysville in the 1930s and had a famous location in Lexington until it closed its doors in 2023. Simple and affordable, it is enjoyed even by those with a more expensive taste. Movie star George Clooney, whose family is from the Maysville area, has been known to share slices of transparent pie on his movie sets. Now we know you want to give it a try.

Copycat Magee's Transparent Pie
1 cup cream
1 teaspoon vanilla extract
1 unbaked (9-inch) pie shell
½ cup (1 stick) butter, melted
2 cups sugar
2 tablespoons flour
4 eggs, beaten

Beat butter and sugar in a mixing bowl. Add cream, and mix
well. Beat in eggs. Stir in flour and vanilla. Pour into pie shell
and bake at 375 degrees for forty minutes or until golden brown.

May Day Pie
1 basic pie dough for single crust (we won't judge you if you use
the store-bought version)

6 large eggs
1 large egg yolk
1⅓ cups dark corn syrup
⅓ cup packed light brown sugar
4 tablespoons (½ stick) unsalted butter, melted
2 tablespoons bourbon (your choice)
1 tablespoon vanilla extract
½ teaspoon kosher salt
2 cups whole pecans, toasted
4 ounces semisweet chocolate chips

Heat the oven to 350 degrees, and place oven rack in the lower
third. Line a 9½-inch deep dish pie plate with dough, and trim
off excess. Bake until the dough is slightly brown, approxi-
mately twenty to thirty minutes. Remove from the oven, and
raise the oven temperature to 375 degrees. Whisk together eggs,
egg yolk, corn syrup, brown sugar, butter, bourbon, vanilla,
and salt in a medium bowl until smooth, about one minute.
Add nuts and chocolate chips, and mix until evenly combined.

Pour into crust, and bake until filling is set, slightly puffed, and dark brown, about thirty-five to forty minutes. Remove to a wire rack, and let cool completely before cutting. Serve cold or at room temperature.

Show: Don't Forget the Benedictine

Benedictine must be the most famous "unknown" food in Kentucky. This spread, mainly made of cucumbers and cream cheese, will be found at any Derby party, racetrack tailgate, or afternoon tea across the state. It was invented around the turn of the twentieth century by Jennie Carter Benedict, a caterer and cookbook author in Louisville. Originally it was used to make cucumber sandwiches, but over the years it's come to be used as a dip or combined with meat on a sandwich.

Born in Harrod's Creek on the outskirts of Louisville in 1860, Benedict began cooking at a young age. In 1893, she convinced a builder to add a small kitchen to her family's home, promising to pay him with the profits from the catering business she intended to start. From this 16 × 16-foot building with no running water, Benedict sold plum pudding, fruitcake, mincemeat, and pulled candies, and she paid that builder back in full. In 1895, she was given the opportunity to attend classes at Fannie Merrit Farmer's Boston Cooking School. By the turn of the century, she had established the Jennie Benedict & Co. restaurant on Fourth Street in Louisville. This community staple had an amazing soda fountain designed with rocks from Mammoth Cave. She catered for former presidents Theodore Roosevelt and William Taft, and she is often celebrated as a champion of the Progressive Era.

Early editions of her *Blue Ribbon Cookbook*, first published in 1902, somehow overlooked her now-famous Benedictine spread, but it's in the most recent one. Benedictine is a not-so-well-kept secret. Celebrity chefs like Paula Deen and Damaris Phillips have whipped up their versions. *Garden & Gun, Southern Living, Saveur Magazine,* and even the *New York Times* and the *Washington Post* have written about the peculiar spread. It's most often made with cream cheese, cucumber juice, onion juice, salt, and cayenne pepper and can be served on crackers, crusty bread, or vegetables.

Benedictine

8 ounces cream cheese, softened
3 tablespoons cucumber juice
1 tablespoon onion juice
Salt to taste
Cayenne pepper to taste
2 drops green food coloring

Thoroughly blend all ingredients with a fork. You may substitute cucumber and onion juices with grated or chopped cucumbers and onions. Serve with crusty bread. Serves eight to ten.

Kentucky Bucket List

We know you're hungry now. Check these food items off your bucket list, and you'll be well on the way to official Kentuckian status.

1. A donut cheeseburger or a hemp hot dog at the Kentucky State Fair. The Kentucky State Fair in August has the finest livestock shows and the most delicious donut cheeseburgers you've ever had. For an alternative, a hot dog infused with hemp will be surprisingly delightful.

2. A German dish in MainStrasse. MainStrasse, a nineteenth-century German neighborhood in Covington, features unique shops and galleries and a variety of great restaurants, beer and bourbon pubs, and venues for live music. The center of the neighborhood, Mainstrasse Village,

offers authentic German food at its Maifest in May and its
Oktoberfest in September.

**3. Tater Days, Ham Fest, the Banana Festival, or another
of Kentucky's great food festivals.** Kentucky has some of the
absolute finest food festivals. There's Tater Days in Benton
and Fulton's Banana Festival (with the World's Largest
Banana Pudding). The International Chicken Festival has the
biggest chicken fryer, and Berea has a celebration of Spoonbread. The Bluegrass State honors barbecue and mushrooms
and pecans and burgoo. Grab your fork and don't miss a
single one.

4. A trip down the Hot Brown Trail. The Bourbon Trail
may be more famous, but following a trail of Hot Browns is
arguably even more delicious. Louisville's Hot Brown Hop
features more than forty establishments. Many serve traditional Hot Browns, but others add ingredients such as ham,
crab meat, avocado, and mushrooms. Some even translate
the Hot Brown into soups, pastas, and seafoods. Other great
food trails in Kentucky include the Donut trail, Candy trail,
Bon Appetit Appalachia, or the State Park Plates Trail (some
of our favorite meals on a road trip have been eaten at the
Kentucky State Park lodges!).

5. A pawpaw from a Kentucky orchard. Anyone who's never
had a pawpaw—not the grandfather kind, the fruit—is miss-
ing out. This sweet and tasty fruit, unfamiliar to many, can
be found throughout the southern, eastern, and midwestern
United States. Pawpaws grow native in Kentucky along the
banks of rivers and creeks or in the undergrowth of a forest.
The large green fruit is heavy and sort of kidney-shaped,
with a tropical flavor reminiscent of, but not quite like, a
mango or banana. George Washington loved them, Thomas
Jefferson planted pawpaw trees at Monticello, and Lewis and
Clark ate them along their travels. The trees fruit in September and October, and you have to be quick or the deer, foxes,

squirrels, and raccoons will beat you to them. Once ripe, pawpaws don't stay good for long.

Suggested Reading

For those whose curiosity (and hunger!) has just been piqued, we include a list of some favorite Kentucky authors and scholars who will offer even more insight into Kentucky's famous culinary masterpieces, and plenty of recipes to try too.

Benedict, Jennie C. *The Blue Ribbon Cook Book*. Lexington: University Press of Kentucky, 2008.

Fox, Minnie C., with Toni Tipton-Martin. *The Blue Grass Cook Book*. Lexington: University Press of Kentucky, 2005.

Lee, Edward. *Smoke and Pickles: Recipes and Stories from a New Southern Kitchen*. New York: Artisan, 2013.

Ludwick, Cameron M., and Blair Thomas Hess. *Famous Kentucky Flavors: Exploring the Commonwealth's Greatest Cuisines*. Bloomington: Red Lightning, 2019.

Lundy, Ronni. *Victuals: An Appalachian Journey, with Recipes*. New York: Clarkson Potter, 2016.

Michel, Ouita. *Just a Few Miles South: Timeless Recipes from Our Favorite Places*. Lexington: University Press of Kentucky, 2021.

Pirnia, Garin. *The Beer Cheese Book*. Lexington: University Press of Kentucky, 2017.

Schmid, Albert W. A. *The Kentucky Bourbon Cookbook*. Lexington: University Press of Kentucky, 2010.

PART 2
MORE THAN JUST BOURBON

The Bluegrass State is universally known for its horses, fried chicken, and bourbon. We could argue that this famous trifecta neglects many of our home state's claims to fame. But, in fact, interest in bourbon is growing rapidly around the globe and with it, our state's reputation for making the best.

Growing up in Kentucky, we often toured bourbon distilleries when visitors came to town—we dipped plenty of bottles in signature red wax and took pictures in shadowy rickhouses among the rows and rows of aging barrels before we ever turned twenty-one. And why not? It's a beautiful way to experience a day in Kentucky. On the way to a distillery, many of which are nestled among the green and woody hills of the Bluegrass and Knobs regions, you may pass working Thoroughbred horse farms, fields of tobacco, and miles of historic rock fences.

The craftsmanship and flavors of America's native spirit are tightly entwined with our culture and history. You might say bourbon runs through our veins. It came to Kentucky with the earliest settlers and is a part of our very foundation.

But please note that Kentuckians don't just drink bourbon. We have a great history of bountiful vineyards—our state was home to America's first commercial vineyard—unique craft breweries, and delicious soft drinks too. And we may or may not know a thing or two about moonshine, but y'all be careful who you tell that to.

Whether you have a taste for the state's famed libation or you're a teetotaler, Kentucky has something for you.

4 | IT ALL STARTS WITH BOURBON (LIKE SO MANY GREAT STORIES DO)

I have never seen a Kentuckian without a gun and
a pack of cards and a bottle of whiskey in my life.

ANDREW JACKSON

We know alcohol isn't for everyone. But, it's hard to write a book about Kentucky without covering the topic of bourbon. Congress designated bourbon as a "distinctive product of the United States" in 1964, and the congressional record later refers to it as "America's Native Spirit." Its history, cultivation, traditions, quality—and, yes, taste—are a matter of fierce pride in this state. Bourbon is Kentucky—whether found along the Bourbon Trail, the Craft Bourbon Trail, or the Urban Bourbon Trail; whether we're talking about the official drink of the "Greatest Two Minutes in Sports" or the preferred toast to a collegiate athletics win. You'll find that bourbon is infused into our lives.

If cocktails or liquor just aren't your thing, or if you're a non-drinker, you'll find no judgment from these Kentuckians. We have some of the best recipes for old fashioned and julep mocktails. Even if you're one of those drinkers who "doesn't like bourbon" (we've heard rumors that these people exist), we still think you'll want to know the basics if you're going to hang around these parts. In a state that has more barrels of bourbon aging in warehouses than it has residents, you'll be expected to know a thing or two about our corn whiskey. In the words of Wild Turkey's longtime Master Distiller Jimmy Russell, "You come for the bourbon, but you stay for the stories. Bourbon tells the best stories."

A Few Things about Bourbon

Bourbon doesn't *have* to be made in Kentucky to be called bourbon, though the best bourbons in the world are made here. While "Kentucky Straight" bourbon must come from the Bluegrass State, the law puts no such restriction on all bourbons. Our legacy, distilling conditions, and recipes are so good that more than 95% of the world's bourbon is made in Kentucky, which often leads to the popular misconception that all bourbon must be made here.

Here's what you need to know to get started on your bourbon education:

1. Bourbon must be made from at least 51 percent corn.
2. Bourbon must be aged in charred, new white oak barrels.
3. Bourbon must be distilled to no more than 160 proof, or 80 percent alcohol by volume.
4. Bourbon must begin aging at no more than 125 proof, or 62 percent alcohol by volume.
5. Bourbon must be bottled at 80 proof (40 percent alcohol by volume) or higher.

Now that sounds like a lot of math and chemistry, but let us put you at ease. You can let all that roll right out of your head unless you plan to open your own distillery. It's more important to learn which bourbons are your favorites. The flavors of bourbon are as unique and varied as the names of Kentucky Derby horses.

Bourbon needs to be more than half corn, but on that base a myriad of flavors can be built, depending on which grains are added. Wheat and rye are the two most common flavor profiles in bourbon. For a sweeter flavor, wheated bourbons are your best bet. If you like things a bit more spicy, you'll probably love a rye bourbon. With practice, you may learn to identify other flavor profiles in your glass: honey, caramel, cherry, cinnamon, and of course, oak. Here's a little cheat sheet of bourbon brands based on flavor (but this in no way covers all of them.)

Corn-forward bourbons: Jim Beam, Evan Williams, Wild Turkey, Knob Creek, Booker's, Old Crow, Buffalo Trace, and Elijah Craig.

Wheated bourbons: Maker's Mark, W.L. Weller, Pappy Van Winkle, Rebel Yell, and Larceny.

Rye-forward bourbons: Basil Hayden's, Kentucky Tavern, Four Roses, Bulleit, Woodford Reserve, Old Forester, Old Grand Dad, 1792, and Very Old Barton.

Give it Some Thought before Starting Your Own Distillery

After all this bourbon talk you may feel ready to mix up some mash and fill a few barrels of your own. But hold on a minute. Gone are the days of bathtub whiskey—bourbon takes a lot more planning and even more time.

Technically, there is no aging requirement for bourbon—it just has to touch the inside of the charred, new oak barrel. But if you stop there, you'll get something akin to a White Dog or moonshine, and not the caramel-colored drink you might be aiming for. Bourbon must age at least two years before it can be called "straight bourbon," and most distillers age their products longer (some say you can't age bourbon too long, but we personally think twelve years is the perfect amount of time for the bourbon to sleep in the barrel).

So how does a distillery support itself while it waits for its first barrels to age? Well, in the meantime they generally distill and market other liquors. Distillers usually start building their brand name with gin or vodka. Some may produce a White Dog variation of their forthcoming bourbon since those are much quicker to make and don't have an aging requirement. But if you're sampling a new company's White Dog, don't think you're getting a taste of what's to come. Sure, it's the same recipe, but don't discount the great influence the barrel and the aging will have on the final product.

Alternatively, more and more out-of-state distillers are turning to Kentucky companies to help custom distill and flavor the first few years' supply of their brand's bourbon until the product in their own barrels ages. Some—and now we're not pointing any fingers over here—distillers that are not based in Kentucky use slightly customized Kentucky bourbons in perpetuity in order to keep that "Kentucky Straight" designation on their bottles.

A History of Bourbon in Kentucky

In colonial America, European settlers drank beer and cider and variations of the Scotch whiskys and Irish distillations they knew from their home country—all more palatable than untreated water. (Did you catch that spelling? "Whiskey" refers to a product made in the United States or Ireland, while "whisky" is used in Scotland, Canada, and Japan.) American corn whiskey was made long before state boundary lines were drawn, when the early colonial governments encouraged corn cultivation. Early settlers discovered that corn was easy to grow and that it made a distinctive, lighter style of whiskey that they preferred to the European malt recipes they had been trying to replicate.

Who made the first Kentucky bourbon? There are conflicting accounts. Some say that General James Wilkinson built a distillery in 1774 at Harrodsburg, Kentucky's earliest permanent settlement, and others say he wasn't even in the state until a decade later. Some say bourbon got its start in Nelson County, and others mention names like Joseph and Samuel Davis, James Garrard, and William Calk. But many overlapping reports agree that Virginia preacher Elijah Craig was the first. In 1787, Craig founded several churches and the first classical school in Kentucky. The entrepreneur and businessman went on to build the first paper mill and the first fulling mill (fulling is a process of washing fibers, usually wool, to remove dirt and oils and create a tighter fabric), and he started a distillery in present-day Woodford and Scott Counties. From preacher to distiller—quite the career change. Georgetown is considered the birthplace of bourbon, and Kentuckians still toast Craig to this day. His namesake bourbon is produced by Heaven Hill Distillery in Bardstown.

If you travel through central Kentucky, just northeast of Lexington, you'll happen upon Bourbon County. Don't get confused—this isn't where that 51 percent corn version of whiskey was first made. The county wasn't named for bourbon whiskey, in fact, it was the other way around. Bourbon County, which was established as part of Virginia in 1785 and then transferred to the Commonwealth of Kentucky in 1792, was named in honor of the French royal House of Bourbon.

Quite a lot of corn whiskey was made and shipped from Bourbon County back in the day. Of course, it wasn't the Bourbon County we know today. The area encompassed about twenty-seven present-day counties, and it contained many distilleries. As barrels of this whiskey were loaded on steamboats for shipping, they received a stamp to indicate their place of origin: "bourbon." Merchants began referring to "barrels of Bourbon," leading to the adoption of the name. Makes you rethink what you write on your luggage tags, huh?

Still, why does the Bluegrass State continue to produce 95 percent of the world's bourbon? Sure, we grow a lot of corn and have to do something with it—you can only eat so much corn on the cob.

But there are more factors that make Kentucky the bourbon capital of the world:

Limestone. Good whiskey comes from the state's geological foundation. Limestone rock stretches under Kentucky's rolling hills, and pristine, limestone-filtered water is key to making the perfect bourbon. With the exception of Alaska, Kentucky has more navigable fresh waterways than any other state in the country, and our distilleries make use of this particular bounty.

Climate. Kentucky's four distinct seasons are also ideal. Bourbon ages in rickhouses with no insulation or climate control. During the warm, humid Kentucky summers, the bourbon is absorbed into the wood of the charred oak barrels and soaks in the flavor. Then the state's cold, but not bitter, winters allow the barrels to retract and release the bourbon back into the barrel. The transition—and the flavors—are incredibly smooth. Visit the distilleries along the famed Kentucky Bourbon Trail and take notice of where each builds its rickhouses and how they are painted. At Wild Turkey in Lawrenceburg, the aging warehouses stand in full sun most of the day, on the tops of the bluffs overlooking the Kentucky River. They are painted white to help repel some of that sunlight—and heat—from the liquor aging inside. At Maker's Mark in Loretta, the rickhouses are located in the shadowed valleys and are painted black in order to absorb more of the sun's heat throughout the day.

Location. Kentucky—with rich land for corn cultivation— fostered the distillation of a new variety of whiskey, and built a booming industry around a drink that we shipped across the United States and, later, the world. When Prohibition began in 1920, five of the six distillers granted licenses to sell medicinal whiskey were based in Kentucky. In 1933, with the repeal of Prohibition and the start of a wartime economy, the Bluegrass bourbon industry was in a great place to come roaring back. That unbroken history of production, plus Kentucky's location—roughly equidistant from Key West, the tip of Maine, and the Colorado Rockies—means that we keep a (loving) stranglehold on our signature export.

Make it Kentucky Straight, and Other Labeling Terms to Know

As we've established, bourbon doesn't have to be made in Kentucky to be called bourbon. But to have the desired "Kentucky Straight" phrase on the label, it has to be distilled and aged for two years in Kentucky. "Straight" means the bourbon in the bottle is at least two years old. There are also other aging statements on bottles, like Pappy Van Winkle's Family Reserve 23 year. If those bottles aren't filled with bourbon from a single barrel, the statement of age is based on the *youngest* barrel. A twelve-year bourbon might have some thirteen- and fourteen-year-old bourbon in there, too!

A label can tell you a lot about what's in your bottle. "Single Barrel" means the bottle was filled from a single barrel of bourbon, and "Small Batch" means the bottle is a blend from a small number of barrels. If you don't see either term, your bottle came from a larger batch of barrels. Don't be put off by that! Blending barrels together ensures consistency, and that means you'll like that particular bourbon bottle after bottle.

You also might see a "Single Barrel, Barrel Strength Bourbon." "Barrel Strength" or "Barrel Proof" means your bottle was filled straight from the barrel and not cut with extra water to limit the alcohol by volume (ABV). Across the Atlantic, where they make whisky, not whiskey, they call it "Cask Strength."

Finally, you might see that a bourbon is "Bottled in Bond." Bear with us as we get a bit technical. The phrase dates back to 1897, when the federal government first started to regulate bourbon. Sketchy distillers and hucksters were adding all kinds of crazy things to whiskey, like turpentine and iodine (yuck!). The Bottled in Bond Act created a federal standard that insured that bourbon was safe to drink. To this day, to be Bottled in Bond, your bourbon must be distilled during a single distillation season of a single year (i.e., January to June or July to December), by one distiller, on one site; it must be aged for at least four years in a government-bonded and regulated warehouse; and it must be bottled at exactly 100 proof. Sure, it's a lot of hoops for the distiller to jump through, but then both maker and drinker can be confident that the final product is top-notch.

A Few Other Terms You Need to Know

If you're going to talk bourbon with a Kentuckian, the key is in the details. Here are a few terms that are likely to come up in conversations at a bourbon bar or retailer, while on a distillery tour, or even just in conversation. What can we say, we know our stuff.

> **Mash Bill:** The recipe of grains that are fermented to create the bourbon. It must be at least 51 percent corn. Catherine Carpenter, a Kentucky frontier woman and pioneering distiller, developed the oldest surviving sour mash recipe in 1818. You can still see the original "original recipe" in the archives of the Kentucky Historical Society.
>
> **Distiller's Beer:** The thick, fermented mash of cooked grains, water, and yeast that is transferred from the fermenter to the beer still for the first distillation.
>
> **Angel's Share:** The bourbon lost through the evaporation process while aging.
>
> **Devil's Cut:** The bourbon that remains in a barrel's staves after it is bottled.
>
> **Rickhouse, or Rackhouse:** The tiered barn or warehouse where barrels age.
>
> **Cooperage:** Where all of those new, charred white oak barrels are made. It is a fascinating process that is worth seeing if you're able! Many of Kentucky's cooperages, including the Brown-Forman Cooperage in Louisville and the Kentucky Cooperage in Lebanon, allow scheduled tours.
>
> **The Bung and the Whiskey Thief:** The bung is a small wooden cork in the side of an aging barrel of bourbon. When you remove the bung to taste and check the bourbon as it's aging,

you use a whiskey thief to "steal" a small amount. Old-fashioned versions of this tool were made of copper and resembled a long drinking straw with a narrow hole at one end and a vent hole to help capture a sample. Modern versions are often made of glass or clear plastic.

How to Sip Bourbon Like a Kentuckian, and a Few Recipes, Too

Most mid- to top-shelf bourbons are what we like to call sippin' bourbons. Depending on your mood, you can "drink it neat"— nothing in your glass—or "on the rocks"—with an ice cube or two. Either way, you'll be sippin' something delicious. If you need more variety than straight bourbon, here are a few suggestions:

One-on-one pairs. Some common delicious mixers for your bourbon that don't require a mixology certificate include ginger ale, cola, and coffee. For a glass full of Kentucky Pride, add Ale-8-One (but more on that later).

The Old Fashioned. Place a sugar cube in the bottom of an old fashioned glass (or you can put a teaspoon of sugar in any thick-bottomed cocktail glass). Moisten the sugar with a few dashes of Angostura bitters. For a bit more flavor, a lot of folks like to muddle a wedge of orange and a maraschino cherry in the bottom of a glass with the sugar and bitters, then add the other ingredients. No muddler? The back of a spoon works great to crush some of the flavor from the fruit. Drop in a few ice cubes and a splash of hot water or soda water and stir with a bar spoon (or a regular spoon, we're not fancy folk). Add bourbon. The precise bartender would call for two ounces. We call for whatever makes you happy and is to your taste.

The Mint Julep. It doesn't have to be Derby Day to enjoy a mint julep, and if you've got fresh mint from the garden in the spring or summer, it sure does make this classic cocktail all the more refreshing. Traditionally, this cocktail is made in a sterling silver julep cup—these used to be given as prizes during county fairs and similar events—but you can use a Collins, highball, or even a larger rocks glass. Muddle a handful of fresh mint leaves in the bottom of your glass to express the flavor. Add a heaping helping of ice (crushed is preferred), ½ ounce simple syrup, and 2 ounces of your favorite bourbon.

The Keeneland Breeze. The other major racetrack in Kentucky is Keeneland in Lexington. Their signature cocktail, the Keeneland Breeze, is a perfect accompaniment to enjoying the spring or fall race meet. Over ice, add 1½ ounces bourbon and 1 ounce of orange liqueur (like triple sec). Top with ginger ale and garnish with an orange slice.

The Hot Toddy. Bourbon is a year-round curative, and there's nothing better than a hot toddy on a chilly evening, or when you're recovering from a winter bug—a Kentuckian's favorite medicine. Add one shot of bourbon to a mug of hot water. Stir in honey, lemon, and/or cinnamon to taste.

If you'd rather drink something non-alcoholic, or if you're not at the right age just yet, there are several ways our favorite bourbon cocktails can be modified:

The Old Fashioned: Try it with your favorite cola or dark soda.

The Mint Julep: Keep the mint and sugar, but use ginger ale or soda water in place of the bourbon. Lemonade is also a delicious variation.

The Keeneland Breeze: Top your ginger ale with a few slices of orange and add a dash of cranberry juice if you're feeling a bit wild.

The Hot Toddy: Frankly, this one is great even if you just leave out the bourbon, but you might find that your favorite black tea also pairs well with the fixin's.

5 | MOONSHINE IN THE BLUEGRASS STATE

Hooch. Rotgut. Shine. Mountain Dew. White Dog. All are names for the same distilled liquor—moonshine. In the past moonshine referred to an illegally distilled American whiskey, but today it is made and sold legally by respected distillers across the country. And if we did happen to know any home distillers working outside the confines of the law, we'd never reveal our sources.

The main difference you'll notice between bourbon and moonshine is the color. Although the distilling process for each is fairly similar, moonshine is not aged in a barrel and is often clear, unlike bourbon, which is caramel brown. In fact, when White Dog, or the alcohol that comes straight off the still, is put into barrels for aging, it is completely clear. Bourbon doesn't get its color until it ages in a charred oak barrel. The other big difference is the mash bill, or recipe. Bourbon must contain at least 51 percent corn, but moonshine and other American whiskeys don't have that requirement.

The glory of today's modern (legal) moonshine is that it can serve as a base for many different flavors and mixers. But before we get into what you can drink today, let's talk about whiskey's colorful past—what was dangerous, illegal, and delicious that you weren't supposed to drink back in the day.

Run for the Hills

Whiskey has had a contentious history in America. Following the Whiskey Rebellion of the 1790s, distillers were angry about the taxes levied on their products. To escape the close, money-hungry eye of the newly formed American government, they moved much of their activity to the Appalachian Mountains. Hidden in the hills and hollers, moonshiners were able to ramp up their production to meet the growing demand of the expanding United States.

During Prohibition, both the bourbon and moonshine industries exploded. Only six legal licenses for "medicinal" whiskey production were issued—remember, five of them were to Kentucky bourbon distillers—but there were plenty more customers looking to get their supply by any means necessary. To cure their ailments, of course.

Aiding the burgeoning moonshine industry were the bootleggers. By the time Prohibition was officially codified in the Eighteenth Amendment, bootleggers, sometimes called rum runners, had become very adept at smuggling 'shine from the hollers and into the cities. And, as the aptly named Roaring Twenties were under way, there was no shortage of demand.

There was, of course, the "small detail" that it was risky to sell and imbibe illegal whiskey. Moonshiners and bootleggers faced many dangers: rival distillers, tricky nighttime excursions through the mountains, and prohibition agents out to destroy the stills and/or the distributors—they didn't care which. Kentucky bootleggers got very good at tinkering around with the newfangled invention called a car. They slimmed down the mechanics, creating space for their crates of bottles, and made sure they could go *fast* to outpace the police and prohibition agents. In their spare time, these early gearheads got to challenging each other to races, and that led to the birth of NASCAR. No, really!

Even after Prohibition ended, folks were still making and selling their own whiskey and 'shine, and the bootleggers were still careening their modified cars around the hills. Future NASCAR Hall-of-Famer Junior Johnson famously earned his learner's driving permit while running hooch, and when the very first race took off at Daytona in 1948, a former moonshine runner named Red Byron took the checkered flag.

Mountain bootleggers were an entire culture and political system unto themselves, and those who took care of the community who supported them were thought of as royalty. The "Queen of the Mountain Bootleggers" was Miss Maggie Bailey of Harlan County. Maggie, who lived to be 101 years old, started selling liquor when she was seventeen to support her family. In her long life of making and selling moonshine, Maggie was brought to court a few times but only ever convicted once, and she served eighteen months in federal prison. Despite the changing times, her alcohol sales remained illegal up until her death in 2005. Harlan County is a dry county, you see.

According to an interview with her longtime friend and lawyer, Maggie was like everyone's grandmother, and no jury wanted to find her guilty. With no children of her own, she looked after her neighbors, gifting food and coal whenever a family needed it. From her simple house in Clovertown in Harlan County, in her simple print dress and apron, she got to know everyone who drove up to her back door for a sale. Her friends said she knew the Fourth Amendment—search and seizure laws—backward and forward, and she kept her own code. She never sold to kids or to "drunkards," as she called them, and she never drank herself. Maggie was beloved in Harlan County, and she was immortalized in the FX series *Justified*, starring Timothy Olyphant. In season 2 of the show, the character Mags Bennett, played by Margo Martindale, was inspired by the legendary Queen of the Mountain Bootleggers.

Nowadays—if you're in a wet county where alcohol sales are legal—you can find moonshine just about anywhere. Many distillers have added moonshine to their lineups, some of it with added flavors such as peach and apple pie, which were popularly infused in mountain moonshine. And high-end moonshine cocktails are served at restaurants and bars. Might it taste better if you had to break the law to get your hands on it? (Of course not.)

6 | THE STUFF THAT ISN'T WHISKEY

Kentucky beverages—the kind with alcohol and the kind without—are not lacking in flavor. With hints of oak and vanilla in our bourbon, citrus and ginger in our favorite caffeinated soft drink, syrupy sweetness in our sweetest sweet tea, and blends of local fruits like the pawpaw (with its tropical mango/banana taste) in our craft beers, we've never been accused of being boring.

So grab your glass and kick up your feet; we have more than just whiskey to impress you with—and that's saying something.

"A Late One"

At any Kentucky rest stop or gas station, you're bound to see Ale-8-One sitting proudly in its iconic green glass bottle among the cold, caffeinated sodas. Nearly one hundred years old, Ale-8-One is a particularly Kentucky quaff. North Carolina can keep its Cheerwine and Maine its Moxie, because we'll stay sipping the Bluegrass State's own gloriously refreshing, highly caffeinated, ginger and citrus soda.

Ale-8, as it's informally known, was first developed in 1926 by George L. Wainscott. He'd been experimenting with another bottled soda he called Roxa-Kola, named for his wife Roxanne, but a lawsuit filed by the United State's largest cola company pushed him to start experimenting with other flavors he could bottle and sell. A research trip to Europe introduced him to the sharp, spicy flavor of ginger beer. He brought the taste back to the States, toned down the spice, added some citrus, and behold! He found the recipe he had been looking for.

Wainscott was working from downtown Winchester, Kentucky. In the spirit of keeping things local, he took his new soda to the 1926 Clark County Fair, where he also sponsored a contest to name the new drink. The winner was a 1920s slang phrase, "A Late One," which loosely translated to "the latest thing." Wainscott liked that—his soda was the latest thing, a gotta-have-it new product. Eventually, the name evolved to its current punny form, Ale-8-One.

Ale-8-One swiftly became a regional hit, allowing Wainscott to build his first bottling plant in an old livery stable in Winchester in 1935. The Wainscott business has since moved to a new plant and has been passed through four generations—current president Fielding Rogers is George L. Wainscott's great-great-nephew. Like his ancestors before him, Rogers hand mixes each batch of Ale-8-One from the original, still-secret recipe in the hometown factory, and each batch is still bottled in Ale-8's iconic green glass (though it's now available in cans, too). No one alive, except for Fielding and his father, knows the exact formula.

We'll tell you more about some of the odd Kentucky turns of phrase in part four. But, for now, in case you're trying to order an Ale-8 in Kentucky, you should know that in most parts of the state, we call every cold, bubbly, non-alcoholic beverage a "coke," whether we want a Coca-Cola or not. Of course, Kentuckians also recognize the terms "soda" and "pop," though it's generally our neighbors to the North saying "pop" and to the West and Northeast saying "soda."

The Sweeter the Tea, the Sweeter the Talk

While both geographically and culturally debatable, many Kentuckians consider themselves southerners, and if you're southern, you take your tea sweet. Extra sweet. You know you're back home when you can just ask for "tea" at a restaurant and you get an iced beverage so sweet that it feels like sugar is coating your tongue and the backs of your teeth. Is there anything better?

The proper way to make sweet tea is to add your sugar while the tea is hot and fresh-steeped; dissolve it in the steaming brew, and then add cold water to dilute to taste. If you add the sugar after the tea is iced, you'll be drinking "sweetened" tea, and there's something about the slight graininess and the imbalance of the tea and sugar that just isn't quite right.

Sweet tea developed in the South in the 1800s and early 1900s. South Carolina first began harvesting tea plants in 1795, and the wealthy southern plantation owners, who could afford sugar and ice, started adding them to their formerly British brews. Alcoholic tea punches also became very popular later in the nineteenth century. In *The Kentucky Housewife*, published in 1839, Mrs. Lettice Bryan's tea punch called for one and a quarter pounds of sugar: "Make a pint and a half of very strong tea in the usual manner; strain it, and pour it boiling on one pound and a quarter of loaf sugar. Add half a pint of rich sweet cream, and then stir in gradually a bottle of claret or of champaign [*sic*]. You may heat it to the boiling point, and serve it so, or you may send it round entirely cold, in glass cups."

Quite frankly, if you just stick with the first sentence of the recipe, then add another pint and a half of cold water, you'd be making a pretty great batch of sweet tea.

If you're feeling particularly lazy and can't be bothered with the whole boiling water thing, or if it gets too hot in your kitchen in the summer months, you can make sun tea like your grandmothers used to. Fill a two-quart or gallon container with water and either four tea bags (for two quarts) or eight tea bags (for a gallon) and set the container out in the sun for three to five hours. When the tea reaches its desired strength, stir in sugar until it dissolves, and place in the refrigerator to cool.

No one can say for sure, but it was probably the Temperance Movement and, later, Prohibition that cemented sweet tea's status as "the house wine of the South," as Dolly Parton perfectly put it in the movie *Steel Magnolias*. When tea punches became non-alcoholic, the sweet caffeination of a black pekoe tea and sugar could still give a refreshing buzz on a hot summer's day. Fortunately, we're no longer under the yoke of Prohibition, so feel free to add bourbon to your sweet tea as you like—our favorite cocktail of this sort is a Porch Swing.

Our Favorite Sweet Tea Recipe. Bring 1 quart of water just past the edge of a boil. Pour the hot water over 6 bags of black pekoe tea (usually Lipton or Luzianne) and steep for 5 minutes. Put 1 cup of white sugar in a large (at least 2-quart) pitcher. Add the hot tea and whisk until the sugar dissolves. Add an additional quart of cold water to the pitcher and stir. For a slight variation, add a handful of mint leaves to the hot water and tea bags as they steep, and strain them out before adding to the sugar.

The Porch Swing. Mix 1.5 ounces of your favorite bourbon with ¾ ounce of lemon juice, ½ ounce of honey, and 6 ounces of peach tea. Garnish with a peach slice or a lemon wheel. Cheers!

Craft Beers, Wines, and Other Bottle Fillers

You've gotta give it to Kentucky, we'll always find a way to bottle our spirit up and share it with the world. We make and export roughly 95 percent of the world's bourbon, and in recent decades, we've also built a reputation for wine, beers, and other tipples and mixers. All of the things that make Kentucky such an amazing place for bourbon production—limestone-filtered water, four distinct seasons, rich soil—make it amazing for vineyards and hops growers as well.

We can actually thank Ben Franklin for kickstarting Kentucky's wine industry. America's founding party boy really loved wine; he wrote the "Drinker's Dictionary" for the *Pennsylvania Gazette* and offered more than 225 synonyms for the word "drunk." Ole Ben loved wine so much that he urged his friend Jacque Rudolph Dufour to send his Swiss-born son, a vintner, to explore the

American West and find a place to establish a winery. When Jean-Jacques Dufour arrived in 1798, he found the soil along the Kentucky River near Lexington to be perfect for growing grapes. Dufour used political connections and local introductions to put together the Kentucky Vineyard Society, a collective of nearly a hundred investors, including statesman Henry Clay (another Kentucky icon), to establish what he named First Vineyard. By 1803, Dufour and his investors were drinking the very first bottles, and they shipped several casks to President Thomas Jefferson. He approved! "The quality . . . satisfies me that we have at length found one native grape . . . which will give us a wine worthy of the best vineyards of France," he said in a letter to a friend.

The third-highest wine producer in the United States in the late 1800s, Kentucky had zero vintners still in operation by the end of Prohibition. But the state is making a comeback and today is home to more than seventy wineries, including Dufour's original First Vineyard. When Tom Beall purchased the property along the Kentucky River, he didn't realize that it was the site of America's first commercial vineyard. On learning the history, he worked to reopen the First Vineyard in 2012 and started producing wines from the very same grape varieties that our Founding Fathers/Party Boys were so eager to drink. From Butler to Hopkinsville, to Verona and Flemingsburg, Kentucky wineries are flourishing.

Kentucky craft brewers have also long been part of the national beer scene, and our state is home to one of the four beer styles indigenous to the United States, although you may never have heard of it. Common beer is a dark cream ale that uses corn and a high content of roasted malts for a flavorful amber brew. The beer originated with the German and Irish brewers who immigrated to the Louisville area. Our fathers used to tell stories about being sent to their local neighborhood bar to grab a bucket of Common for their fathers when they were younger. The Kentucky Common was recently revived by Louisville's Falls City Brewing. Today, we can all click our glasses in "Cheers!" for a great tradition brought back to life.

Secret Recipes

Since we're all Kentuckians here, we'll let you in on some of our best secret drink recipes that will impress all of your guests.

The Best Brunch Bloody Mary/Maria/Marianne

We like a Bloody Mary with *allll* the fixin's for a weekend hair-of-the-dog brunch, so you'd better believe we're going to dress up a bottle of mix with some extras. To a big pitcher, add the following:

1 750-ml bottle of your favorite bottled Bloody Mary mix, Clamato, V8, or plain tomato juice
1 teaspoon prepared horseradish
1 tablespoon Worcestershire sauce
1 tablespoon black pepper
1 teaspoon celery salt
A few dashes of hot sauce to your taste

Serve over ice with a shot of vodka, tequila, or bourbon, as you like. Throw in your favorite, most outlandish garnishes—maybe it's a strip of caramelized bacon, or extra olives, or celery, or even cocktail shrimp. There are very few rules when it comes to brunch.

Bourbon Smash

An evolution of the classic Kentucky mint julep, a bourbon smash adds a crushed handful of seasonal fruit or berries. We especially love a smash when sipping out on the porch in the summer. We also love to top our smash with a squeeze of a lemon or a splash of ginger ale or Ale-8-One.

In the bottom of a heavy glass add and muddle:

A few sprigs of mint
A tablespoon of sugar or 1 ounce of simple syrup
2 slices of a seasonal fruit, like peach, melon, or grapefruit

-OR-

A small handful of seasonal berries like blackberries, blueberries, or cherries

After muddling together, add ice, 2 ounces of bourbon and any garnish you might want to use.

Whiskey Sour

Making a whiskey sour is the Kentucky equivalent to the bartender's daiquiri test—there are few ingredients, but if you don't hit the balance just right, you'll find yourself serving a sour note and not a sweet and sour treat. Many classic recipes call for the addition of an egg white when shaking up your cocktail to make it extra frothy. We don't think that's necessary, but it's awfully fun and fizzy.

In a cocktail shaker without ice, add:

2 ounces bourbon
¾ ounce fresh-squeezed lemon juice
½ ounce simple syrup or a teaspoon of sugar
1 egg white, if using

Give it a quick shake, then add ice and shake like a wild thing until everything is well chilled and frothy. Strain into a cocktail glass, or into a fresh Collins glass with ice. Add a cherry for garnish, or if you like an old-school vibe, add a few drops of Angostura bitters on top instead.

The Kentucky Golfer

We Kentuckians love our sweet tea, and we're just as happy to let it share a glass with lemonade, á la Arnold Palmer, the King. But, add some bourbon, and your cocktail skills will get you an approving clap from the gallery.

Palmer's preferred blend was three parts unsweetened tea to one part lemonade; we prefer equal parts of each. This is one of

the few occasions when we'll keep our tea unsweetened; both bourbon and lemonade add sugar.

Over ice, add 2 ounces of bourbon and your Palmer-esque blend. Add a wedge of lemon and stop stressing about your backswing.

Kentucky Bucket List

Let's keep adding to that bucket list. To experience some of the best Kentucky drinking around, here's where we suggest you start.

1. Tour one of the state's bourbon distilleries. The Official Kentucky Bourbon Trail, the state's Craft Bourbon Trail, and the Urban Bourbon Trail, along with the many great distilleries that stand alone, offer tours. You can see how bourbon is made, from grain to bottling, and hear great stories of the master distillers and the families who have kept these brands growing. And don't worry, there's a taste test waiting for you at the end.

2. Tour the Ale-8-One Factory in Winchester. Ale-8-One has been producing its ginger soda for over a hundred years in Winchester. You can tour the plant and bottling facility to see how the delicious soft drink is made. Just don't expect them to spill the century-old secret Wainscott-Rogers family recipe!

3. Head to Bardstown for the Kentucky Bourbon Festival. This annual festival mixes black-tie events with golf outings, hot rod runs, and family fun. Oh, and there's a lot of bourbon to drink there, too. Each September, Bardstown's normal population of thirteen thousand more than triples for a week. The six-day event is held rain or shine—wear your boots if it rains, it gets muddy—and offers smooth bourbon, great food, entertainment, and good old-fashioned Kentucky hospitality.

4. Discover one of Kentucky's craft breweries or wineries. The first vineyards in Kentucky are actually some of the oldest vineyards in the country, dating back to the 1700s! First Vineyard in Nicholasville claims to be the oldest vineyard in the United States. And Baker-Bird Winery, in Augusta, is home to the oldest, largest wine cellar in the country. It is forty feet wide, forty feet tall, and ninety feet deep.

5. Make your own simple syrup for mint juleps. We promise, it's easier than it looks! If you can boil water, you can make simple syrup. After all, it says "simple" in its name. This sugary ingredient is key to making a delicious mint julep (a drink consumed by more than 120,000 Derby-goers every year on the first Saturday in May). Mix half a cup of granulated sugar and half a cup of water in a small saucepan over medium heat; stir until the sugar is dissolved and let cool. Voila!

Suggested Reading

To learn more about bourbon and moonshine (and the milder stuff, too), and for more recipes (you can never get enough!), here is some recommended reading from Kentucky authors and scholars.

Carson, Gerald. *The Social History of Bourbon*. Lexington: University Press of Kentucky, 2010.
Crowgey, Henry G. *Kentucky Bourbon: The Early Years of Whiskeymaking*. Lexington: University Press of Kentucky, 1971.
Kentucky Bourbon Trail. https://kybourbontrail.com/.
Kentucky Distillers Association. https://kybourbon.com/.

Ludwick, Cameron M., and Blair Thomas Hess. *The State of Bourbon: Exploring the Spirit of Kentucky.* Bloomington: Red Lightning, 2018.

Mauer, David W. *Kentucky Moonshine.* Lexington: University Press of Kentucky, 2003.

Minnick, Fred. *Bourbon Curious: A Tasting Guide for the Savvy Drinker with Tasting Notes for Dozens of New Bourbons.* Boston: Harvard Common, 2019.

Mitenbuler, Reid. *Bourbon Empire: The Past and Future of America's Whiskey.* New York: Penguin, 2016.

Risen, Clay. *American Whiskey, Bourbon & Rye: A Guide to the Nation's Favorite Spirit.* New York: Union Square, 2015.

PART 3
BIG HATS COME RAIN OR SHINE

While Kentucky is, in fact, home to Paris, London, Athens, Versailles, and Rome, none of these Bluegrass towns come to mind when folks talk about fashion. But Kentuckians sure do have their own sense of style, and it, much like the Bluegrass State way of life, is rooted in culture and history.

From Daniel Boone's raccoon-skin cap and Abraham Lincoln's stovepipe hat to Daisy Buchanan's flapper look and the outlandish, creative outfits seen on that distinctive race day in May, fashion has always been a way to connect to the character of a particular place and time. Unfriendly stereotypes might describe a Kentuckian as a shoeless redneck wearing overalls, a straitlaced, booted horse person, or a prissy blonde in a floral dress with unmistakably "southern" accessories. And yes, we're all that, but we're also so much more!

These Kentucky girls love any excuse to get dressed up, but there's a reason we wear big hats to the Kentucky Derby. We wear our lipstick bright and our foam fingers with pride while cheering on our favorite teams, and there's a history there too. Kentucky is home to glamorous trailblazers of fashion, historic and innovative weavers, and more than a few fashion oddities.

It isn't just about how you look (though, we find a little fun in that part, too). Dressing like a Kentuckian means observing some of our favorite pastimes, celebrating some of our earliest creative types, and honoring a few regional influences while we're at it. If anything, we can at least teach you how to tie that pesky bow tie.

So, strap on those riding boots and saddle up. You'll be dressing like a Kentuckian in no time.

7 | THE BIGGER THE DERBY HAT, THE CLOSER TO GOD, AND OTHER KENTUCKY DERBY FASHION TIPS

"We're going to have a picnic at the racetrack." As he went door-to-door, the founder of the Kentucky Derby, Colonel Meriwether Lewis Clark Jr. (grandson of explorer William Clark of Lewis and Clark Expedition fame), tried to attract Louisvillians to his brand-spanking-new racetrack. You see, in the 1870s, racetracks were viewed with suspicion as places where gambling, drinking, and carousing often went hand in hand; Clark's invitation to a picnic was an attempt to portray the track as a spot where high society would socialize, a place suitable for women and children.

Clark was the son of Abigail Prather Churchill. The Churchill family had moved to Louisville in 1787 and bought three hundred acres of land south of the city. When his mother died, the young Clark moved to Louisville to live with his aunt and her sons John and Henry Churchill. They had inherited most of the family's land, and they donated some of it to Clark to build a racetrack.

Clark became famous for throwing extravagant parties—he had developed a taste for expensive things living with the Churchills—and it wasn't long before he took an interest in horse racing. But he envisioned it in a venue that would appeal to the city's most stylish residents. During his travels in Europe in the early 1870s, he visited England's Epsom Downs racecourse, home of the Derby Stakes. This was a 1.5-mile race for three-year-old horses that was organized by the 12th Earl of Derby and his rich friends. Having seen that horse racing could be a classy affair, Clark founded the

Louisville Jockey Club and planned a racetrack where bookmaking, typically used at tracks, would be replaced by a French system, parimutuel betting.

In Louisville, Clark worked to make his investment pay off. He had a plan. He rounded up some of his well-to-do female friends and they went from house to house telling their acquaintances to get dressed up and head to the races. Clark wanted to make the brand-new Churchill Downs a place of fashion, and nothing screamed high society like great clothes.

More than ten thousand spectators attended the first Kentucky Derby on a sunny spring Monday in 1875. Clark was proved right. Although it would be a few years before the Derby turned into a celebrity affair, fashion was as famous as the morning line, the hats and handbags were discussed as much as the odds and winner's purse. The women coordinated their hats, dresses, bags, shoes, and parasols, and, just like that, horse racing became a regal affair.

So why big hats? In the early years, they were products of the times, both functional and fashionable. Leghorn hats, large white felt hats, and straw hats helped block the late spring sun and protected the ladies' eyes and skin. In the late nineteenth and early twentieth centuries, fancy hats were an expected part of a woman's outfit. The really large and over-the-top styles finally started to appear in the twentieth century. In the 1960s, when social fashion norms relaxed a bit, and as the growing broadcast television networks turned their focus to the first Saturday in May, the hats also grew in size—to stand out in a crowd, of course.

In the 1980s, Derby hat fashion evolved again. In 1981, Prince Charles married Lady Diana Spencer and all eyes turned toward England for a royal wedding, which featured a parade of fancy hats and fascinators. These became popular with Derby-goers who wanted to don a smaller (though no less fabulous) accessory. Today, unique hats and bold spring prints are a must-have for ladies attending the Kentucky Derby. So how do you pick a hat? And where on earth do you find such a piece of art?

You don't have to visit a milliner to find a great Derby hat, although many do. The average fancy hat can cost from $300 to

$500, and some of these masterpieces cost thousands. But your local department store will have a perfectly acceptable (and much more affordable) Derby hat.

Choosing the Perfect Derby Hat

A quick note: Our discussion and tips may sound geared toward women, but they apply equally to men! Men's hat fashion at the Derby is just as creative and crucial as the women's.

Pick the hat first. Many fashion pros will tell you to pick the dress and then find a perfect hat to match. But trust us—the hat needs to come first. Come on, y'all, this is the Kentucky Derby! It is all about the hat. Pick one you love, that fits and is comfortable to wear all day, and then find a dress, shoes, and accessories to match. Everyone notices the hat first anyway.

It is a statement, so let it stand out. Let the hat be the star of the show on Derby Day. It is the one occasion when even people who never wear hats will wear hats. Make the rest of your outfit minimal so that it doesn't steal the show.

Make sure it is something you can leave on all day. If you're attending the Kentucky Derby, you'll be spending most of your day outdoors. And honestly, most Derby parties are outside as well, so your hat can stay put. Make it something that is comfortable—not too heavy—that you'll be okay with sporting all day. Also think about what you have planned and the weather forecast. If you're going to be in direct sunlight, make sure your hat has a wide brim to shield your eyes. Going to the infield? Maybe a more subtle hat is a better choice. Is it going to rain? Avoid feathers or veiling, which don't hold up in damp conditions, and watch out for dyed hats. Some colors will run and streak your hair.

Plan your hair around your hat. If you have shorter hair, it is OK to leave it down. But for folks with hair longer than shoulder length, we recommend pulling it back into a low updo to keep it out of your face and looking great, even after long hours outside.

Think about your height. If you're tall, don't assume you can't sport a big hat. The taller you are, the bigger hat you can support. Have fun with size and shape. Consider a wider brim. If you're short, don't wear a brim that droops down on both sides. Try an asymmetrical brim that goes down on one side and up on the other.

Buy something you can wear again. We know, we know. They always say, "You can wear it again!" and they never, ever mean it. But really, maybe you can. Pick a great wide brim straw hat and dress it up with a very fancy bow in a sparkling spring color. Then after the Derby, pull off that ribbon and wear the hat to the beach this summer.

Go the DIY route. Some of the most memorable hats at Churchill Downs each year are those that are homemade and fancy free. Don't be afraid to dress up a simple topper with your own Derby-inspired diorama, horsy motifs, or whatever crafts come from your wildest imagination. We've seen pink flamingos, architectural re-creations of the Twin Spires, and every possible color feather, flower, and fabric. Remember Olympic figure skater Johnny Weir's 2015 hat? It came with its very own mint julep!

Don't stress about etiquette. When it comes to your fabulous Kentucky Derby hat, let's just assume you're going to put that thing on in the morning and take it off at the very end of your day. Whether outside in the infield, on the paddock, or in the grandstands, or if you happen to wander indoors for a few minutes, your Derby hat can stay firmly planted on your head. It is an exception to other hat rules.

Pastels and Seersucker, but Never White

The Kentucky Derby takes place the first Saturday in May each year, when the weather is perhaps the most unpredictable. Will it be cool? Will it be hot? Is it going to rain? The answers: Yes, yes, and likely, yes. So, we don't have to tell you that as delightful as Derby fashion is, it can be almost impossible to plan. Our advice: make it bright and bold, and wear layers that can come off and go back on easily. Derby fashion celebrates fun spring colors and patterns, so embrace the season and do the same. Men and women alike wear pretty pastel colors, and there is hardly a better place to debut your favorite seersucker.

Seer-whater? Seersucker. The fabric is woven on twin looms at different speeds, which results in its puckered look. Most commonly striped—traditionally a pale blue and white—and sometimes checkered, seersucker is a common textile for spring and summer clothes, often in pastel colors. The fabric's name originated in India as *shir o shakka* (Persian for "milk and sugar") because it appears to have a smooth part (milk) and a rougher part (sugar). British traders in the seventeenth century changed the name to seersucker, which was easier for English speakers to pronounce.

One final fashion tip for Derby Day: avoid white. Not only would Emily Post frown on white before Memorial Day (save it for summertime, y'all), but from a practical standpoint, you're just asking for trouble wearing pristine white to an outdoor horse race. Forget the animals and the dirt, you're bound to be bumped by a passerby and spill a drink or drop a little burgoo while eating in your lap. No one needs that added stress.

The Art of Tying a Bow Tie

Ah, the bow tie. This debonair, typically dressed-up fashion statement takes on an outdoor, daytime form at the Derby, perhaps in a classic seersucker (see above) version or in a madras or other festive spring pattern. If you can find one with little, tiny, embroidered horses, roses, or horseshoes, well, you've hit the jackpot.

The downside of a bow tie? With such great fashion sense comes great responsibility: you must know how to properly tie and wear your bow tie. Pre-tied? Clip-on? Absolutely out of the question. And a bow tie that is too loose or too crooked really ruins the effect. So, here's an important life skill, a rite of passage even. Learn how to properly tie a bow tie.

1. Hang the bow tie flat around your neck, pulling one side (side A) longer than the other side (side B) by about an inch to an inch and a half.
2. Bring side A across side B close to your neck to prevent the tie from becoming too loose.
3. Continue to bring side A up behind side B, forming a simple and loose knot.
4. Fold side B to make a bow tie shape by pulling it to the left and then folding it back over itself to the right. The fold should be directly between the collar points of your shirt.
5. Drape side A over the front of side B.
6. Fold side A and pass it through the loop behind side B.
7. Continue pulling side A through the loop without pulling it completely through. This will form the back half of the bow.
8. Tighten the knot and adjust until even, by pulling on opposite sides simultaneously. Pull the front left and the back right section to tighten. Pull the front right and back left end apart to loosen.
9. Look up the video tutorial and replay 100 times.

Kentucky Derby Tips and Tricks

Aristides won the first Kentucky Derby race in 1875 with a time of 2 minutes and 37 seconds. He was ridden by Oliver Lewis, an African American jockey, and was trained by renowned African American trainer Ansel Williamson. The Derby, the longest-running sports event in the United States, is commonly called the "Greatest Two Minutes in Sports." More than 150,000 people come to Churchill

Downs each year to drink mint juleps, sing "My Old Kentucky Home," wear their big hats and bow ties, and bet on the ponies. How proud Colonel Meriwether Lewis Clark Jr. should be.

In part one of this book we told you about the culinary influences of the Derby; in part two, we recommended some great drink recipes for the occasion. We'll let you in on a poorly kept secret: we're going to be telling you a lot about the Kentucky Derby throughout this guide. (Look ahead to part four for more tips on celebrating.)

In truth, many Kentuckians go to the Derby once for the experience and after that only if they're escorting a curious visitor. If your budget doesn't stretch to getting grandstand seats or a box, buy paddock tickets and spend the day watching the horses before they run and trying to spot celebrities on Millionaire's Row. Avoid the infield at all costs unless you're really, really brave, and don't mind not having a view of the race. Kentucky native Hunter S. Thompson's classic essay, "The Kentucky Derby Is Decadent and Depraved," was mostly narrated from the infield. That experience inspired gonzo journalism,  which should tell you a lot about the vibe you'll find there.

If you plan to celebrate the Derby from a distance, throw a party (see part four) and invite all of your friends—we've celebrated the Run for the Roses in New York, in Texas, and even in an airport bar! Make your own simple syrup and offer mint juleps in fancy cups alongside other cocktails. Place bets and do blind horse draws out of a jockey hat. And make sure to watch on TV, so everyone can sing "My Old Kentucky Home" and yell "Go, baby, go!" for the "Greatest Two Minutes in Sports."

While Kentuckians may skip the in-person Derby experience after going once, many frequent the Kentucky Oaks, a slightly more casual affair and one of our favorite traditions. At the Oaks, held the day before the Derby, the fillies get to take the spotlight for a race that's every bit as exciting as its more famous brother.

This special race has its own customs. Guests wear pink in support of the fight against breast and ovarian cancer and there is a Survivors Parade before the race. It is customary to sip on the signature Pink Lily cocktail while you watch the girls compete for a blanket of lilies.

8 | FAN OUTFITTING

A WHOLE DIFFERENT BALL GAME

Fewer than half of the US states—Kentucky among them—are without one of the "Big Four" professional sports teams (National Football League, National Basketball Association, Major League Baseball, and National Hockey League). Kentucky did, at one time, have a professional basketball team: the Kentucky Colonels. The Louisville team was part of the American Basketball Association for all nine years of its existence, from 1967 to 1976. Basketball has always been great in Kentucky, and the Colonels won the most games of any franchise in the league, 448. When the American Basketball Association merged with the National Basketball Association team in 1976, the Colonels chose not to join the NBA. The team won the ABA Finals in 1975 and was disbanded the following year along with the ABA. Colonel stars Dan Issel and Louie Dampier, both former University of Kentucky Wildcats, were known for their three-point shooting and were inducted into the Naismith Memorial Basketball Hall of Fame.

Even without a professional sports team, Kentuckians are passionate about athletics. The Bluegrass State is home to one of the most heated rivalries in college basketball, and the state shares the famous southern devotion to football.

Kentuckians have enough game day gear and enthusiasm to extend to all sports—we're happy to cheer on the University of Kentucky national championship rifle team with enthusiasm any day. But when we think about dressing for game day, those sunny fall weekends outside of a football stadium are always top of mind.

Perhaps it was Hall of Famer Marino Casem, longtime coach at Alcorn State and Southern University, who said it best: "On the

East Coast, football is a cultural experience. In the Midwest, it's a form of cannibalism. On the West Coast, it's a tourist attraction. And in the South, football is a religion, and a Saturday is the holy day."

We had a teacher once who referred to Kentucky football game days as "a sublime Southern psychosis." It seems fitting. The excitement has been shared by all those who have ever posted up under a tent on the blacktop outside of UK's Kroger Field, sat on the grass in the endzone at Eastern Kentucky University's Roy Kidd Stadium, visited the Alley across from the entrance to UofL's Cardinal Stadium, or met on the Hill in Bowling Green, the home of Western Kentucky University. While, arguably, many aspects of Kentucky culture and customs have roots in the Midwest, on game days Kentucky has a deep pull to the South.

After the Civil War, the North continued to urbanize and develop economically and industrially. The southern states—Kentucky included—remained more rural and agrarian well into the twentieth century. So, it's not surprising that as pro football teams began to pop up in major cities across the Northeast and Midwest in the mid-1960s, the South didn't land any such teams. As a result, we clung to the college version of the sport tighter than ever before. And when we cling, y'all, we cling in style.

It's important at this point to properly introduce you to tailgating. The American Tailgater Association says the practice of tailgating started at the first intercollegiate football game—Princeton vs. Rutgers in 1869—when spectators gathered to grill sausages at the "tail end" of a horse. It may have started earlier: this country has been cheering for its favorite "team" since its earliest days. In 1861, civilians gathered near Manassas, Virginia, to watch the First Battle of the Bull Run—the first major confrontation of the Civil War—and to cheer on their team: the Union or the Confederacy. Those people, with their picnic baskets filled with minced meat and plum puddings and whiskey and dressed in their very best, were effectively tailgating the battle. Before you call this morbid, just consider how you cheer when your favorite defensive lineman plows into the opposing team's quarterback and choose your words wisely.

How to Dress for a (Any) Tailgate

Oh, sure, you may think you've been tailgating before, but in Kentucky we have worked to perfect the practice. We go all out here and will tailgate absolutely anything.

Like most seasons in Kentucky, fall is characteristically unpredictable. Here in the Bluegrass State, we like to joke that it could be 80 degrees one day with a low of 42, chance of thunderstorms and possibly 2 inches of snow tomorrow. You wish we were kidding. Since tailgating takes place outdoors and goes on for many hours, here are a few dos and don'ts of dressing for an old Kentucky tailgate:

DO *dress in layers.* It's easy to adjust to changes in unpredictable Kentucky weather if you have a few options. Wear a T-shirt or collared shirt under a sweater, pair a team T-shirt with a light jacket. Check to see if you'll be on the shady or sunny side of the stadium. Trust us, it makes a big difference in temperature!

DON'T *involve face paint.* We're passionate fans too but leave the face paint for someone else. It's itchy, it's cakey, and it's the first thing to come off on your favorite team-color shirt. But foam fingers are always OK.

DO *accessorize.* It's the most fun part of your game day outfit! Choose a team-logo needlepoint belt and your favorite hat (for looks and functionality in that bright October sun). And don't forget your earrings and necklaces sporting your favorite team mascot and colors.

DON'T wear heels. Wear a dress if that's your thing—there's nothing wrong with dressing up for game day. But leave the heels at home. You'll be standing (at the tailgate and to cheer on your team!) and walking a lot. Plus, you never know what's going to get dropped on your feet in a stadium. Ew!

DO consider pockets. Pockets are always good, but on game day they're a necessity. If your jacket, vest, or dress has pockets, you may be able to avoid bringing a purse into the game.

DON'T pack a big purse. No one wants to lug a heavy bag around a tailgate, and you'll never make it through stadium security with the thing. If you don't have enough pockets, choose a clear tote or a clear crossbody bag—they're available in some fairly stylish options. And check the stadium rules before you bring your bag to the gate—the trek back to your car to stow your bag can be a long one.

As previously stated, Kentuckians don't restrict tailgating to just Saturday football games. We love a good picnic after church, a game of cornhole in the fields outside of Keeneland Racecourse, and even a front yard snack while watching a couch burn after a basketball victory. But more on that later.

9 | WEAVERS, MONOGRAMS, AND FRINGE, OH MY!

Kentucky may not come to top of mind as a leader in fashion (although we are home to our own Paris and London, thank you very much), but certain fashion truths are universally understood across the state. Even Daniel Boone was quite the fashion icon—have you seen his racoon skin hats? What about the fringe on his coat and boots? We love a little fringe.

Here are a few fashion tips from these traveling Kentuckians:

If it's not moving, monogram it. Shirts, jackets, purses, shoes, coffee mugs—you name it, let's put some script initials on it, y'all! When the logo of the Southeastern Conference looks like a monogram, you know the style is a full-on way of life. Monogramming is rooted in the Kentucky—and southern—tradition of embroidery. Young children (male and female) are taught the skill, and many of us grew up in households filled with embroidered towels, wall hangings, pillows, napkins, and you name it. And hey, it is a stylish way of staking your claim on stuff. Plus, you'll keep it forever.

Put your face on. Now, this can mean a full face of beauty-parlor-acceptable makeup or just your game face. Growing up, we were taught that no Kentucky girl could have too much mascara, blush, or lipstick—rules we still live by today. We think that putting your face on doesn't diminish what's under the surface. Just think of the suffragettes—they wore red lipstick to show their solidarity. A trip to the beauty shop doesn't make you any less strong or independent, it just gets you ready for what's ahead.

Choose the appropriate boots. Contrary to the whispers, Kentuckians do actually wear shoes. And boots! There are boots for every occasion—cowboying, motorcycling, horseback riding, a night on the town. But use some judgment—don't show up to saddle your Thoroughbred in your run-of-the-mill cowboy boots. And don't you dare head out to the field to cut the tobacco crop in your riding boots. This isn't the Wild West, y'all!

Kentucky's Most Glamorous Women

Salvador Dali painted her portrait. Truman Capote modeled the character of Kate McCloud in *Answered Prayers* after her. Cole Porter had Ethel Merman sing about her in *Ridin' High*. Vogue called her "extraordinary catlike eyes and blue-grey hair a New York phenomena." But, before she was named "The Best Dressed Woman in the World" by a panel that included Coco Chanel, Mona von Bismarck (born Mona Strader in Louisville in 1897) was just a Kentucky girl who was raised on a horse farm in Lexington.

Mona married five times. The first time was in 1917, to Henry Schlesinger, the owner of Lexington's Fairland Farm, where her father worked as a horse trainer. Over her life, Mona opened a New York dress shop, married one of the richest men in America, Harrison Williams, and had homes on Fifth Avenue, in Palm Beach, in Capri overlooking the Marina Grande, and in Paris at the famous Hotel Lambert. She also wed Albrecht Edzard Heinrich Karl, Graf von Bismarck-Schonhausen (she called him "Eddie"), the grandson of German chancellor Otto von Bismarck.

In 1933, Mona was named "The Best Dressed Woman in the World" by Chanel, British fashion designer Edward Molyneux, French fashion designer Madeleine Vionnet, French couturier Lucien Lelong, and French fashion designer Jeanne Lanvin. She was the first American woman to receive that honor, and in 1958 she was named to the International Best Dressed List Hall of Fame.

She died in 1983 and was buried—in Givenchy, of course—on Long Island with husbands Three and Four. Today, the Mona Bismarck American Center for Art and Culture in Paris works to foster artistic and cultural relations between France and America—quite the legacy of Kentucky hospitality.

Another feather boa–wearing beacon of Kentucky fashion, the late Anita Madden, was married to Thoroughbred horse giant Preston Madden, who owned Hamburg Horse Farm in Lexington. Anita was most famous for holding lavish parties on the eve of the Kentucky Derby each year for four decades, from the mid-1950s to the late-1990s. She was perhaps equally as renowned for her extravagant fashion.

Anita's Derby parties were always decadent—we know this from friends and friends of friends who were lucky enough to get a peek into a few; we were never lucky (or old) enough to be on the guest list—and her outfits at the events were just as unforgettable. She once wore the 111.59-carat Earth Star diamond, on loan to her for the event from the De Beers company. Another time, she sported a cape decked out with hundreds of purple feathers. One of her most memorable parties, with the theme "Arabian Nights," featured hydraulic lifts used to make it appear as if people were flying on magic carpets. Can you even imagine?

The event grew and grew, each more dazzling than the one before it. Along with her local friends and family, guests included movie stars, authors, athletes, politicians, and other celebrities who mingled among the horse industry crowd. Media outlets including Entertainment Tonight, The Today Show, and VH-1 covered Anita's galas and their fashionable red carpets. The last event, held in 1998, had more than three thousand guests. (We'll tell you more about these lavish experiences in part 4.)

Anita was also known across Kentucky for her commitment to her community. Her annual gala was a fundraiser for The Bluegrass Boys' Ranch, which helps prepare young boys for higher education. Anita and her only son, Patrick, helped transition the charity into the scholarship program it is today. Anita served on her local planning and zoning commission, and Governor John Y.

Brown appointed her to the Kentucky Horse Racing Commission, where she served as the state's first female racing commissioner from 1980 to 1983.

The horsewoman and philanthropist died in 2018 at the age of eighty-five, and you can be sure we scoured some of her estate sales and the local secondhand stores looking for any of the clothes that were sold. We came away with a few scarves, one handbag, and the most fabulous pair of mules you could imagine (even if we did have to squeeze into that size 7.5). Not all were feathers and rhinestones, but all were fabulous. Today, the commercial corridor Hamburg Place in Lexington, which Anita and her son helped develop, sits on the family's former horse farmland. It has roads named for the famous race winners Sir Barton—the first Triple Crown winner—and Alysheba.

Mona and Anita were trailblazers, not only fashionable but also enterprising. They are just two of the countless fashionable

women from all races, backgrounds, and social and economic standings across the Commonwealth who have left their mark on our state's arts and culture.

Meet the Famous Churchill—Not the Racetrack—Weavers

Kentucky is a trove of fun and sometimes surprising history just waiting to be discovered. For example, in 1960, during the lead-up to Project Mercury, the first human spaceflight program in the United States, a husband-and-wife team of weavers at a Kentucky company were asked to produce an anti-thermal fabric for NASA. Churchill Weavers made fifty yards of special fabric that was considered (although not chosen) for use in coveralls for astronauts to wear over a pressurized high-altitude suit. You probably can't find a Churchill Weavers spacesuit today, but a visit to eBay or other secondhand shops may offer an opportunity to purchase a baby blanket or throw made by the company.

David Carroll ("D.C.") and Eleanor Franzen Churchill started Churchill Weavers in Berea in 1922. They wanted to bring employment to the Appalachian region, and they shared a passion for high-quality handwoven fabrics. With handweaving looms designed and built by D.C. Churchill and fabric designs created by his wife, Eleanor, it was the first company to mass-produce handwoven products for a national market.

D.C., a native of Ohio, studied engineering at the Massachusetts Institute of Technology; Eleanor came from Connecticut and was a graduate of Wellesley College. They traveled together to India, where D.C. worked as an engineer with the Marathi Mission, which was affiliated with the Congregational Church. In the early twentieth century, handweaving was the second-largest industry in India, and the couple were entranced by the craft. A talented engineer with a few inventions under his belt, D.C. developed a fly-shuttle loom that allowed weavers to produce twice as much cloth.

The Churchills landed in Berea after D.C. received an offer from Berea College to teach physics. He planned to build a business in his free time that would focus on designing and selling looms to handweavers. But as they built their home in Berea, D.C. and Eleanor decided to produce handwoven goods themselves. Churchill Weavers, best known for its baby blankets and larger throws, also produced clothing that they marketed nationally.

The family ran the company until Eleanor sold it in 1973, four years after D.C. died. Churchill Weavers continued to produce handwoven items until it closed in 2007. Its reputation for craftsmanship added further to what was already community tradition; Berea has been a bedrock of Kentucky's arts and crafts scene for more than a century. Today, the town is often referred to as the Folk Arts and Crafts Capital of Kentucky.

Kentucky Bucket List

Pick out your best Derby hat and mark some items off of your bucket list—Kentucky has a little something for everyone. Whether you head to the racetrack or a tailgate or make your way to an arts and crafts fair or a battle reenactment (yes, you read that correctly), don't be afraid to dress the part!

1. Camp out on the Paddock at Churchill Downs and watch the celebrities arrive. We're talking about the Derby horses *and* the Hollywood crowd! The actors, athletes, and models will cross the Paddock and head for Millionaire's Row. The horses competing in the Run for the Roses will relax on the Paddock before the famous race. You're not a Kentuckian until you've spent a day in the sun on the Paddock with a mint julep in hand.

2. Tailgate on the hill at Keeneland in Lexington. Sure, the Derby is a big deal and all, but you haven't experienced horse racing until you've spent a day at Keeneland. Founded in 1936 and located smack in the middle of the Bluegrass region, Keeneland sits among some of the most famous Thoroughbred breeding farms in the world. Its annual September Yearling Sale has produced more than twenty Kentucky Derby winners, more than twenty Preakness winners, and nearly the same number of Belmont Stakes winners. Keeneland is picturesque and serene—it was the perfect location for the movie *Seabiscuit*—until the opening gates release and the horses run. Wear your horse racing finest—a season-appropriate dress or trousers for the women, a sport coat and bow tie for the gentlemen—and spend an afternoon under the shady oak trees in Lexington. Keeneland meets run weekly in April and October each year (no racing on Mondays, Tuesdays, or on Easter Sunday).

3. Throw cornhole at a college football or basketball game. Some say that cornhole was actually first played in Kentucky.

No, really! Cincinnati may claim that it was first played there in the 1960s, but many enthusiasts say the game dates back to the fourteenth century. Others say that pioneers in the mountains of Eastern Kentucky played "baggo"—a game of tossing bags of corn at holes in the ground. Well, never mind where it started, dress in your favorite game-day gear (remember, pockets, clear bags, flat shoes, and team colors!) and throw a few bags ahead of your favorite college team's big game.

4. Attend a battle reenactment and check out the Civil War–era costumes and camps. As a border state in a strategic territory, Kentucky saw fierce contests between the Union and the Confederacy during the Civil War. Add that the presidents of the North and the South—Abraham Lincoln and Jefferson Davis—were both born in Kentucky and you get a state that has deep ties to the war conflicts. Kentuckians love a good Civil War battle reenactment (another reason to tailgate!). The Battle of Perryville is one of our favorites. The largest battle on Bluegrass soil, and one of the bloodiest of the war, Perryville cemented the Union's control of our border state. The reenactment takes place in early October each year (bring lots of water, October is surprisingly hot in Kentucky) on the actual ground where the original battle was fought. Around two thousand reenactors dress in authentic Civil War–era uniforms and camp out in true-to-the-times camps during the annual commemoration. Dedicated to the details of their outfits, these men and women are definitely some of Kentucky's best dressed.

5. Celebrate the spirit of Kentucky Artisans and the Churchill Weavers in Berea. While the historic handweaving company shut down in 2007, many of its products can still be found at secondhand stores, antique malls, and online sites like eBay. You can see many Churchill Weaver creations at the Kentucky History Center in Frankfort. And the Kentucky Historical Society owns the Churchill Weavers archive of more than thirty thousand textiles, which includes nearly a complete representation of every Churchill Weavers weave pattern. Of course, the state is home to other craftsmen as well. At the annual Berea Craft Festival each July, more than a hundred artists bring their work, and many provide demonstrations.

Suggested Reading

The way Kentuckians dress has roots in Appalachian and southern traditions, among others. To learn more about fashion influences on the Bluegrass State, here's some suggested reading.

"Betty D. Eastin Collection: Anita Madden Collection," University of Kentucky Libraries. https://libguides.uky.edu/c.php?g=222999&p=4820792.

Birchfield, James D. *Kentucky Countess: Mona Bismarck in Art & Fashion.* Lexington: University of Kentucky Art Museum, 1997.

"Churchill Weavers Collection," Kentucky Historical Society. https://www.kyhistory.com/digital/collection/Weave/search.

"Derby Fashion," The Kentucky Derby: "Run for the Roses." The Filson Historical Society. https://filsonhistorical.omeka.net/exhibits/show/kentucky-derby/derby-fashion.

Nicholson, James C. *The Kentucky Derby: How the Run for the Roses Became America's Premier Sporting Event.* Lexington: University Press of Kentucky, 2014.

Ownby, Ted, and Becca Walton. *Clothing and Fashion in Southern History.* Oxford: University Press of Mississippi, 2020.

Rice, Rebecca S. "The Mona Strader Bismarck Collection," *Filson News Magazine* 4, no. 3, https://filsonhistorical.org/archive/news_v4n3_MonaBismarck.html.

Spence, Jennifer. "The Churchill Weavers Collection: An American Treasure Uncovered," Proceedings of the Council on Library and Information Resources Cataloging Hidden Special Collections and Archives Symposium, March 2015. https://www.clir.org/wp-content/uploads/sites/6/spence.pdf.

PART 4
A GOOD REASON FOR A SHINDIG

We hope by now you've seen how committed Kentuckians are to their history, culture, and traditions. And what better way is there to demonstrate your passions or to honor the things you love the most than with a celebration?

It should be no surprise that the South knows how to throw a good party, and Kentucky sure is part of the South when it wants to be. Here in the Bluegrass State, the land of bourbon, basketball, and 'breds (Thoroughbreds, for the uninitiated), there's no lack of occasions, and we're just waiting for an opportunity to play host.

There are glittering, star-studded Derby parties, boisterous tailgates at the football game and at the horse track, street corners packed with revelers after a big game, Main Streets filled with homegrown food vendors, parks rocking with music festivals, and plenty of good old-fashioned open houses for holidays, baby showers, weddings, and more.

More than just an excuse to party, Kentucky festivals are a convergence of family, friends, community, and tradition. We celebrate where we come from, where we are, and where we might go. Sometimes we get together around food, sometimes we express ourselves through music or art, sometimes we meet to remember our history. There's no better way to get to know a state than by observing—and joining in—the very things its people celebrate.

Sadly, we've yet to figure out how to package a bottle of bourbon and a platter of Benedictine inside of a book. But, hey, if you ever want to host us for a dressed up or a dressed down hootenanny, we'd be happy to bring something along.

10 | THE FASTEST TWO MINUTES IN SPORTS

Y ou'd think we might get tired of talking about the Kentucky Derby eventually. After all, we've told you how we dress for it, we've told you what we eat when we're there, we've discussed the best cocktails and mocktails for the occasion and what you might think to be *all* the ins and outs of an event that lasts a mere 120 seconds. You might think that. But you'd be wrong. There's always another special secret we can let you in on.

The Kentucky Derby Festival is, without a doubt, the biggest celebration in Kentucky. Over the roughly 150 years that the Derby has run, Kentuckians have figured out how to stretch a two-minute race into a full two-week celebration. And really, why wouldn't we? It has something for everyone—no matter where you come from, what you can afford, whether you care about the outcome of the horse race, or even which kind of whiskey you favor—beautiful horses, food, cocktails, long-standing customs, wild fashion, and wilder hats.

These days more than seventy events lead up to the "Greatest Two Minutes in Sports," including fireworks, boat races, hot air balloons, and concerts. Heck, you can even get yourself invited to a ball—the fancy dress-up-and-dance kind—in Louisville, which transforms fully into Derby City in the weeks leading up to early May each year.

The Kentucky Derby Festival: A Celebration Like No Other

The Kentucky Derby Festival has a glorious kickoff: Thunder Over Louisville is the largest annual display of fireworks in the United States. Roughly two weeks before Derby Day (or three weeks, if it conflicts with Easter), the festivities start with a BANG.

Since 1989, "Thunder" has rocked the city with both an air show and after-dark fireworks display. On average, more than 600,000 people line the Ohio River—on both the Louisville and southern Indiana sides—to see thirty explosive minutes of light, color, and music. More than sixty thousand shells are launched from eight four-hundred-foot barges and along the full span of the Second Street George Rogers Clark Memorial Bridge.

It's one thing to watch an incredible fireworks display on television. It's quite another to stand underneath the bridge and to *feel* your body shake from the inside out and to realize that the soft flakes falling on your face are bits of ash.

At the very first opening ceremonies of the Derby Festival, twenty thousand multicolored balloons were released (we're super sorry, Ozone Layer, we didn't know better back then). As daytime fireworks shells were set off for the crowd of about ten thousand, someone asked if it would be possible to have the event at night. What a great idea.

These days, you'll want to snag the annual Pegasus Pin to show vendors for discounts and special incentives at events during the festival. Each year, pin purchases help subsidize the events and help local retailers bring in the community; they offer deals just for participants. With a pin purchase, you might even win one of the weekly prizes or the grand prize cash giveaway!

The Pegasus Parade, the festival's oldest event and one of the largest annual parades in the United States, leads up to the Derby. Other notable traditions include the bed races, hot air balloon show, and the historic steamboat race. There's no shortage of activities, with a little something for everyone!

The Races

After all the initial fanfare, there still is a race to be run on the first Saturday in May. Each year, twenty horses qualify to run in the Kentucky Derby, one of the most sought-after races in the industry. In a process something like *Survivor* for Thoroughbreds, the horses undergo a series of challenges to reach Churchill Downs. Here's what each must do to be a Derby contender:

The horse should be three years old. This is why the Kentucky Derby is known as a once-in-a-lifetime event for horses—you're only three once, right? This rule is in place so that the competition is fair—in theory, at least, horses of the same age will have similar power and agility.

The horse needs to run some prep races. Practice makes perfect. A horse has to run in prep races designed by the Derby organization in order to gather points. Each of the thirty-five races gives out points to the top four finishers. As the Derby gets closer, the points on the prep races increase, giving more significant points to the top winners. Horses with a minimum of forty points can enter the Kentucky Derby race. These prep races are run in New York, California, Louisiana, Arkansas, Florida, Oklahoma, and Kentucky. You might remember Rich Strike's historic win in 2022. The colt hadn't qualified for the field of twenty before the race; he was twenty-first and that was only because of a "show" finish a mere four weeks before the Derby. But when one of the originally qualified horses withdrew the day before the 148th Run for the Roses, Rich Strike got his moment to win the second-largest upset in Kentucky Derby history.

There's a Wild Card. Because OF COURSE there is! We have to keep y'all on your toes! The final race of the Road to the Kentucky Derby prep races, the Lexington Stakes held at Keeneland, offers a score of 20–8–4–2 to the top four winners. It's a huge opportunity for contenders to earn additional points to qualify.

Pay up. The teams that want to run a horse in the Derby have to pay an entry fee ($25,000) and a starting fee ($25,000). That's after they pay the early nomination fee or the late nomination fee. Y'all, it ain't cheap; but rest assured, if they win the Derby, these teams will get a lot of money. They just have to fork over a little first.

Of course, the Kentucky Derby is only just the beginning. Since 1930, the winner of the Kentucky Derby can go on to run the Preakness Stakes in Maryland and the Belmont Stakes in New York. A horse that wins all three in the same season is designated a Triple Crown winner, the highest honor in horse racing. As of 2023, only thirteen Thoroughbreds have won the Triple Crown. Invite us to trivia night—we can name all thirteen!

We know, it's a lot. But you really have to wrap your head around the enormity that is the Kentucky Derby and all that's riding (no pun intended) on the event. Once you grasp that, you can understand why Kentuckians hold this time-honored tradition so near and dear and why we go all out when celebrating each year.

A Little More History While We're at It

First run in 1875, the Kentucky Derby was born from the horse racing traditions of England. Earlier, we told you about Meriwether Lewis Clark, grandson of the famous American explorer William Clark, who loved his experience at the Epsom Derby in Britain so much that he wanted to create a signature American Thoroughbred race back home in Louisville. His cousins John and Henry Churchill, gifted him with the land that first became the Louisville Jockey Club, which raised the capital to build a permanent racetrack. Aristides, ridden by African American jockey Oliver Lewis, beat out fourteen other Thoroughbreds in that first Derby and took home the $2,850 purse (equivalent to about $76,000 today).

Whether an every-year tradition or a one-time memory maker, a trip to the actual race at Churchill Downs can be an overwhelming experience: crowded, hot, cold, rainy, dusty. Many Kentuckians find it a little too packed with tourists or with the party people of the infield to be truly enjoyable. So instead, they go to the Oaks, which takes place on Friday, the day before Derby Day on Saturday. At the Kentucky Oaks, the "Fillies Run for the Lillies."

Although there is no rule about it, the Derby is traditionally run by male horses. But the Oaks is reserved for the three-year-old fillies. A heavily pink-colored affair, the Oaks features multiple "Ladies First" events, including a parade for survivors of ovarian and breast cancers, and fundraisers for Louisville's Norton's Cancer Institute. Both the Oaks and the Derby have been run continuously since 1875, making them the longest contested sports events in the United States. (The Derby was, technically, delayed twice, but it was still run in the designated year. In 1945, World War II delayed the event; and in 2020, the COVID-19 pandemic pushed the Run for the Roses to September.)

A bit newer to the scene, and certainly an insiders' event, is Thurby. Held on the Thursday before the Oaks on Friday and the Derby on Saturday, it is attended mostly by locals. This pre-Derby celebration is a bit more relaxed and laid back, with no wild crowds and no dress code: dress to the nines, or simply wear jeans and a T-shirt with no judgment from your fellow Louisvillians.

Favorite Traditions

Some Derby traditions have been around since the start, some are more recent. We're big fans of them all, old or brand new. Here are a few of our very favorites:

Roses. The "Run for the Roses" got its name for the locally made blanket of roses (usually composed of more than 450 blooms) awarded to the Derby winner each year. The Derby has been awarding roses since 1896, when Ben Brush received an arrangement after his win. Today, this blanket of roses even gets its own police escort to Churchill Downs.

Hats. A hat at the Derby is not just practical—keeping sun, wind, and rain off your face—it is your biggest statement of fashion and personality. If you missed our hat tips in part three, retrace your steps and check out our helpful tricks.

Mint Juleps. A mint julep may be enjoyed any day of the year, but on Derby Day, you almost certainly will find the signature cocktail in your hand at some point. Roughly 120,000 mint juleps are sold at Churchill Downs each Derby Day, using more than ten thousand bottles of bourbon, one thousand pounds of fresh mint, and sixty thousand pounds of crushed ice. Multiply those numbers with the Derby parties held among the estimated 15 million television viewers, and you can raise a glass to the Kentucky Derby with fans all over the world.

Betting. Yes, betting can be complicated. "Churchill Downs. 12th race. $10 exacta box on 8 and 7." Sounds completely baffling. Fortunately, there are easy straight bets and plenty of just-for-fun versions of at-home betting pools to let everyone feel the high stakes of the "Greatest Two Minutes in Sports." For the beginner who's just looking to say they put some money on the Derby, the most straightforward is a $2 bet for your horse to win, place, or show. A bet to win is a bet that the horse will come in first place; to place, that it will come in first or second. To be "in the money" with a bet to show, your horse can come in first, second, or third. Derby parties may feature plenty of variations on a classic betting pool, and we'll get into a few of those later on. In part five, we teach you the language and how to use a racing form so you can talk like you belong at the track.

The Infield. The Derby is defined by its glitz and glam. However, if you are more "of the people" than the type to be seen on Millionaire's Row, you might find that the Churchill Downs infield is the place for you. This standing-room-only crush in the center of the track's oval was immortalized in Kentucky-born writer Hunter S. Thompson's iconic essay, "The Kentucky Derby Is Decadent and Depraved." As Thompson puts it, the infield is "a fantastic scene—thousands of people fainting, crying, copulating, trampling each other and fighting with broken whiskey bottles." He wrote the essay in 1970, but we can't say that much has changed. There may be a bit more control amongst the horde, and bourbon and other corporate spirits brands have looked to tame and commercialize the "decadent and depraved" infield experience; still the ethos remains the same. If you snag your tickets to the infield, we recommend plenty of sunscreen, sturdy shoes or boots, and water to stay hydrated. You also shouldn't expect to see the race, except via the giant TV screens set within the oval, while you stand shoulder to shoulder with your fellow cheering Derby enthusiasts.

Prepare for the Weather

"Neither snow nor rain nor heat nor gloom...." Wait, that's not it. While the Kentucky Derby doesn't officially hew to the US Postal Service motto, the race must go on, no matter the weather. For those lucky enough to have covered seats in the grandstand, the mercurial weather of a Kentucky spring isn't usually too much of a bother. But if you're in the auxiliary bleachers, the paddock, or the infield, you'd better be dauntless and prepared. The first Saturday in May can range from 50 to 80 degrees Fahrenheit, and it's a coin flip as to whether or not it'll rain. Nearly half of all Kentucky Derby days since 1875 have seen rain at some point—in 2018, almost three inches of rain fell on more than 157,000 spectators between 1 and 7 pm. So, that was fun. And soggy.

The smart Derby-goers come prepared. The easiest, most versatile tool at your disposal is a clear trash bag—you still want to show off your hat and outfit! A trash bag easily wraps around a large Derby hat to tuck securely underneath a brim, and three strategic holes at the bottom can turn the bag into a poncho over your outfit; umbrellas aren't allowed at Churchill Downs during Derby week. If you're in the grandstand with a jacket or bag you don't want to hold, a trash bag can shield and protect your belongings from spilled drinks or food. (This also one of our favorite tips for storing your things under the bleachers at a football or basketball game.)

We recommend a few simple styling tips to keep your Derby Day from becoming a struggle. Tights or panty hose can help women stay warm during the chilly morning or evening, and, paired with a static guard, can help prevent wardrobe malfunctions with dresses or skirts. A cardigan and/or coordinating jacket is a must for layering as well as styling. And, we're fans of adding a large silk scarf; depending on how it's used, it can keep the wind and chill off your neck, poke out of your jacket as a pocket square, or tie on to the strap of your bag for an extra pop. The same jacket rule applies for men. Most men wear a hat but, if they decide not to, they should bring a pair of sunglasses along.

The Most Famous Parties

If you plan on throwing your very own Derby party, we have lots of ideas below to help you plan a soiree fit for your family and friends. But first, there are plenty of notable Kentuckians you can turn to for inspiration. And nothing quite compares to two of the most legendary parties of all: the Barnstable Brown Gala in Louisville, which still takes place today, and the former Derby Eve Party put on by Anita Madden in Lexington.

In part three we told you a little about horsewoman Anita Madden and her extravagant fashion, but now we'll keep our promise to give you a better picture of her Derby Eve parties. Picture this: it's 1991 and an engraved invitation invites you to Hamburg

Place Farm for the "Rapture of the Deep"—hosted by Lexington socialite, philanthropist, and racing royalty, Anita Madden. At the expansive and luxurious family home on the twenty-thousand-acre farm, you're greeted by mermaids and mermen and a giant octopus surrounded by dry ice fog. In a grand entrance, the hostess descends the stairs on the arm of her good friend, actor Dennis Cole. The legendarily flamboyant Madden wears a sultry mermaid dress with a three-foot bronze tulle train. The invitation noted that guests should dress "as bare as they dare," and Anita's décolletage is framed by sparkling gold and bronze faux fish scales, her midriff swathed with bronze fishing net. Atop her head is a crown that would make Amphitrite jealous—a gold and bronze oyster shell nestled in a tiara of pearls with blue and turquoise anemone-like flowers flowing from the top.

We so didn't make this up. It's hard to overstate the astonishing aesthetics of Anita's joyous collection of Derby Eve outfits—they have their own archive and occasional gallery exhibitions—as well as the dazzle of her fetes. Madden's parties never disappointed, with themes such as "Land of the Midnight Sun," "The Fun Also Rises," and "The Ultimate Odyssey." During the latter, the Trojan War was reenacted beneath a sixteen-foot statue of Zeus holding a neon thunderbolt. Anita's husband, Preston Madden, was a breeder and trainer; he was heir to his grandfather's farm, which had bred more than one hundred stakes winners. The couple hosted their fabulous party for nearly forty years, from the mid-1950s until 1999, when Anita's mother passed away. The legacy of their hospitality lives on. Hamburg Pavilion is a commercial and residential development with street names that honor notable racehorses, like Sir Barton and Alysheba, who were bred and trained on the farm. And Anita's annual party raised funds that continue to endow charities. Her gala often benefited the Bluegrass Boys' Ranch, but many other charities throughout the region also benefited, including AIDS initiatives, the Kentucky Heart Fund, and Just Fund Kentucky.

The Maddens entertained many celebrities of the seventies, eighties, and nineties. Today, the Barnstable Brown family has taken on the glittering mantle of Derby hosts. Twins Patricia Barnstable Brown and Priscilla Barnstable have been hosting their Derby Eve gala in their capacious family home in Louisville's Highlands neighborhood since 1988; Condé Nast named the event one of the Top Ten parties in the world. The daughters of infamous University of Kentucky basketball star Dale Barnstable, Patricia and Priscilla (also known as "Cyb") rose to fame as the Wrigley's Doublemint Gum Twins in advertisements in the 1970s and, later, as Playboy Bunnies and recurring guest stars on *Quark,* a sci-fi television series. They are local celebrities, and their annual Derby gala is a hot ticket that gets hotter every year. Sports stars like Patrick Mahomes, Tom Brady, and (University of Kentucky fan favorite) Randall Cobb, along with other star athletes from Kentucky universities, rub elbows with actors like Chris Pine, David Alan Grier, Dennis Quaid, and Paula Patton, as well as musicians (all genres), business magnates, and other celebrities, from Jeff Bezos to Prince Albert of Monaco. At $1,500 a ticket and rising, the gala benefits the Barnstable Brown Center for Diabetes Research at the University of Kentucky as well as an endowed chair.

Just down the street from the Barnstable Brown Gala, a lesser-known, but just as consequential, party was first celebrated at Shirley Mae's Cafe and Bar in 1989. The Salute to Black Jockeys was a tradition that continued for nearly a decade. Shirley Mae Beard had opened her restaurant and juke joint the year before in Smoketown, the first African American community in Louisville. By creating a Derby event to shine a light on the contributions made by Black jockeys to the Kentucky Derby, she and her family hoped to inspire and celebrate their local community.

The major impact of Black jockeys and trainers in horse racing has rarely received the acknowledgment it deserves; their impressive achievements are something to celebrate. Here's some background history so you'll understand why this party was such a very big deal in Louisville. In the first Kentucky Derby, thirteen of the fifteen riders were Black men, and eleven of the first fifteen winners of the Kentucky Derby were Black jockeys. The early Derby was trained, jocked, raced, and won by former slaves and

Black men employed by the wealthy white Thoroughbred owners. Racism, stoked by *Plessy v. Ferguson* and Jim Crow laws, began to push Black horsemen out of elite racing; after 1921, no Black rider saddled up in the Kentucky Derby until Marlon St. Julien in the year 2000. But in the early days of racing, perhaps the best-known and most popular hero was Isaac Burns Murphy, the first jockey to ride three Derby winners. In 1891 Murphy rode Kingman, the first and only Derby-winning horse trained and owned by a Black man, Dudley Allen. Isaac Murphy was one of the highest paid athletes of the time—of any race—and still holds the highest winning percentage of any jockey in American history, a record that will probably never be surpassed. He was in the first class of inductees to the National Museum of Racing and Hall of Fame.

Shirley Mae's daughter, Chef Teresa Beard, paid a visit to the Kentucky Derby Museum, where, in the basement, she discovered the names and photos of those eleven Black jockeys who won fifteen of the first twenty-eight Kentucky Derby races. The incredible stories of these jockeys, including Oliver Lewis who rode the first Derby winner, Aristides, needed to be told and celebrated in a big way. So, Shirley Mae started the Salute to Black Jockeys and grew it into the largest inner-city carnival in the state. She fiercely protected its location in Smoketown despite efforts of city officials to move the event to a more affluent locale.

As the Beard family put it, "The Salute to Black Jockeys has all of the stars and no money. And the Kentucky Derby Festival has all of the money and no stars." Shirley Mae's Cafe attracted big names like Whoopi Goldberg, B.B. King, and Morgan Freeman, as well as sponsors like the Coca-Cola company, the Louisville *Courier-Journal,* and other local businesses, which kept the event in its original location and free to the community. The party is no longer held each year, but Shirley Mae's Salute to Black Jockeys program lives on. She's been featured in national media and was instrumental in getting the Kentucky Derby Museum to add its exhibit honoring Black jockeys, which opened in 1995. And those photos that Shirley Mae's daughter found in the basement all those years ago are now prominently featured in the museum.

How to Host a Derby Party

Now that you've been briefed on just a few of the state's most impressive Derby soirees, you're ready to throw your very own Kentucky Derby party. Any great party has key elements—food, drinks, decoration, and good company. A Derby party also includes a special southern spirit. We've felt that spirit at Derby parties not just in Kentucky, but across the United States and even once at an airport bar. Maybe it has to do with the compression of a huge amount of anticipation, participation, and joy into two minutes. Maybe it's feeling connected to more than 150 years of tradition and sharing a few minutes simultaneously with people around the world. Or maybe the gentility of classic southern hospitality makes a partygoer feel like a king (or queen) while watching the Sport of Kings. Whatever it is, a Kentucky Derby party just hits different.

Let's start with the food and drink. Heavy hors d'oeuvres and a few classic southern snacks will keep everyone sated, and of course, mint juleps (virgin or not), bourbon, and sweet tea should stock the bar.

The Menu

The best eats for an at-home Derby fete are bite-sized, sweet, and savory, perfect for snacking on throughout a long afternoon and evening of race watching. We recommend southern and Kentucky classics like Burgoo, biscuits, and Benedictine (see part one). For now, consider the following sample menu:

- Beaten biscuits and country ham
- Burgoo (recipe in part one)
- Pimiento and beer cheese dips
- May Day pie (see part one)

Your Bar

A well-stocked Kentucky bar usually comprises bourbon, bourbon, and more bourbon, and okay, maybe a few ryes too. And nonalcoholic versions of distinctive Derby cocktails welcome nondrinkers to join in toasting the Derby horse who makes it to the Winner's

Circle. For more about bourbon, see part two of this book. We'll sort you out with some Derby party drinks:

- Virgin mint julep
- Arnold Palmers (with or without booze)

The Best Bets

Now for the fun part: let's win you a little bit of money. What's a Derby Party without some friendly wagers? Whether the bets are official or not, you'll want your guests to be all-in on the result of the Big Race. Watching the race is a jolt of excitement when you have a horse to root for. One of the easiest methods is to have your betting guests contribute to a pool, then draw the names of the Derby entrants randomly from a hat. You could also ask guests to "wager" on a horse they predict will win—if there are multiple wagers on the winning horse, the bettors split the prize. If you have *lots* of participants, say, as for an office pool, the classic game Squares can be adapted with the Derby horses listed vertically (to win) and horizontally (to place). Purchase a square as an exacta bet, and the winning square will take home a sizable pot!

The Decor

Of course, good friends and good cheer are all you need to have a great time, but a few roses won't hurt the vibe. You could go all out to create a lush photo backdrop of boxwoods and roses, or accordion-fold some red tissue paper into rosettes that can be taped, hung, or scattered around. Plenty of party stores these days are selling plastic jockey hats and faux silver julep cups (or real ones if you're extra fancy). And, if you happen to have a hobby horse, we can attest that a ride around the party is massively popular with both kids *and* adults.

11 | HANGING NATIONAL CHAMPIONSHIP BANNERS

Kentuckians really like winning, and we've gotten used to it thanks to the amazing performances of our collegiate athletes. Nothing beats a winter trip to a bowl game or that moment in an arena, with cheers reverberating around you, as you watch another championship banner raised into the rafters. You won't find many professional sports leagues making a home in Kentucky—the collegiate athletes are our professionals, and they make us just as proud as any professional league ever could.

The University of Kentucky boasts eight men's Division I basketball national championship titles, and the University of Louisville has claimed two. Put those together, and Kentucky is just one shy of UCLA, which has eleven, the most of any program. Basketball aside, UK boasts championships in volleyball, rifle, cheerleading, cross country, and yes, even one football championship in 1950. UofL also claims success across their teams in volleyball, dance, soccer, and football.

You might also recognize a few of our other successful collegiate athletics programs. There's Murray State in Western Kentucky, whose Division I basketball team consistently appears in the NCAA tournament and claims multiple regular season and conference tournament championships in the Ohio Valley Conference. The Division III Transylvania University Pioneers in Lexington regularly hold the Heartland Collegiate Athletic Conference Women's All Sports Title, as well as athletes of the year in Women's Basketball and Golf. And in what may be an obvious fact to

Kentuckians who grow up with hoop dreams, every single one of the twenty-six colleges and universities in the state that fields teams in the NCAA sponsors both a men's and women's basketball team.

We love to cheer on our teams, whether from a tailgate on a beautiful fall day or on the road to the Final Four. We celebrate victories in style and welcome our athletes home with signs and enthusiasm when their planes touch down or their buses pull in.

Although Kentuckians are united in our dedication to our teams, in our respective fandoms, we do tend to get a bit, well, divided. Some Kentuckians we know cheer for other teams—their favorites in the NBA or the stars they follow in the NFL. Some even cheer for out-of-state or nearby-state college teams. But any Kentuckian knows that even though you can have additional loyalties, come time for the big games, you're going to have to declare an allegiance to one of two teams: Cardinal or Wildcat.

A Spirited Rivalry

Kentucky college sports fans are passionate, dedicated, and completely loyal to their respective teams. No, seriously: once a Kentucky Wildcats fan receiving treatment at a dialysis center was punched by a Louisville Cardinals fan—there for the same reason, mind you—following a heated discussion about the impending 2012 NCAA Final Four game. Yeah, that happened. Kentuckians aren't shy about pinning the hopes and dreams of an entire state on the backs of a few (very talented) eighteen-to-twenty-one-year-olds playing a game.

Across all sports—but particularly with basketball and football—hard lines are drawn between team loyalties, and it is rare to see a fan of one team cross over to the other side (we have seen it happen, but it is sort of like seeing a miracle or a unicorn or something else that just doesn't make sense to exist in the real world).

So no, Kentucky doesn't need a professional sports team. These two university squads are so dominant, so beloved, and so polarizing (for better or for worse), we have enough to keep us busy in the world of athletics. The rivalry between Kentucky and Louisville is ranked among the most intense and heated in American athletics, and the two have a history of finding friction in every possible way. This rivalry is rooted in a historical division, and the separation runs deep enough to still impact us today, even if many in the state have no memory or knowledge of it.

The University of Kentucky was founded in 1865 as a land-grant institution. The Morrill Act, passed by the US Congress, provided funds to establish land-grant schools, which were to teach "agriculture and the mechanic arts." While the university also offered education and research in other fields and later expanded to add medicine, pharmacy, and engineering, most of the first students came from farms in the rural parts of the state. They traveled to Kentucky for scientific training in agriculture that would improve their farming operations. (Some people need reminding that farming is about more than cows and sows and plows and that the folks who run these essential businesses are no country bumpkins.) In contrast, the University of Louisville was founded several years earlier, in 1798, in Kentucky's most urban community. It was the first city-owned public university in the country and was one of the first universities chartered west of the Allegheny Mountains. (Transylvania University in Lexington, chartered in 1780, is the oldest institution of higher learning west of the Allegheny Mountains.)

There is a natural divide between the two schools—one with ties to rural communities and one founded in the heart of the most urban area—which reflected the division between the cultural mindset of the "Old South" and the urbanism of the "New South." With the start of the Jim Crow era, these divisions deepened along with racial tensions. The University of Kentucky didn't allow Black students to enroll in its undergraduate programs until Lyman T. Johnson sued the school in 1948, but the University of Louisville had been educating African American students through its Louisville Municipal College since 1931.

In the 1930s, Adolph Rupp—you might recognize that name for the arena named for him in downtown Lexington where the Wildcats still play basketball today—was the head coach of the UK men's basketball team. Often called the Baron of the Bluegrass, Rupp recruited 80 percent of his players from in-state and, with his Kentucky good ole boys, led his teams to 876 wins across his forty-one years of coaching. Rupp's four NCAA tournament victories, numerous conference titles and head coaching accolades, and induction into the Naismith Memorial Basketball Hall of Fame and the College Basketball Hall of Fame all testify to his skill and success as a coach. But he wasn't as great at recruiting Black players.

In 1964, Westley Unseld became the first Black player offered a basketball scholarship to the University of Kentucky. Community leaders in Lexington worked hard to bring him to UK, but in the end, Wes committed to play for the University of Louisville, which was already integrated. The NCAA tournament his sophomore year saw the first-ever all African American starting lineup, fielded by Texas Western University, who famously defeated the all-white lineup of Adolph Rupp's University of Kentucky. Then the University of Louisville became the second collegiate team to start five Black players and make it to the Final Four. After he graduated, Wes was selected as the second pick of the NBA draft in 1968.

UK would eventually get there. The widespread integration of college basketball began in the 1950s, and UK basketball started to recruit Black players in 1960. In 1969, Tom Payne became the first African American to sign a scholarship to play basketball for Kentucky, recruited by Coach Rupp. He stayed just one season before declaring for the NBA's hardship draft. In 1972, Joe B. Hall, who had played for Coach Rupp in the 1940s and had recently joined his coaching staff, recruited a six-foot, sharp-shooting leftie named Reggie Warford, who would become the first Black player to graduate from UK. Rupp retired in 1972, and Joe B. Hall was named head coach of the Wildcats. Under Hall, the first five Black players to make a Final Four appearance for the Wildcats took the court together in 1975.

As is so often the case with deep systemic problems, many Kentucky and Louisville fans alike don't realize that their spirited rivalry has roots that run so deep. It's hard to believe now, but before the 1990s, the teams rarely faced off, so rivalry between their fan bases took place off the field and court. UK and UofL were in different regional conferences, and there was no reason to set an annual game between the two teams—in basketball or football. The traditions and legacies of each school had roughly seventy years to build before UK and UofL started to meet regularly on the basketball court. We're not exaggerating when we tell you that a ticket to that game is the most exclusive, most expensive ticket you can buy in the state. The competitive spirit is so fierce, that when the University of Louisville basketball team signed a contract to make the KFC Yum! Center in downtown Louisville its home court, they stipulated that the University of Kentucky team was never allowed to play a game there unless it was during an NCAA tournament or against Louisville themselves.

Basketball reigns supreme in the Bluegrass State. But many Kentuckians also consider themselves southerners, so football is not to be disregarded in this rivalry. In the 1990s, the two schools established the Governor's Cup football game. Initially this was the very first game of the season for each of the teams; now it is played in the climactic final weekend of the college season, usually around Thanksgiving. What bigger thing do we have to be thankful for, y'all? Along with bragging rights, a custom silver trophy is passed between the teams and engraved with that year's winner.

The Home Team Advantage

When we say Kentucky is big on sports, we mean big, and we don't need a professional stadium to prove it. Just look at the seating capacity and attendance numbers of our home games. The Louisville Cardinals play their football games at Cardinal Stadium to a crowd of sixty-one thousand. As a point of reference, only four cities in Kentucky have populations over sixty-one thousand. This stadium, when full, would be the fifth-largest community in the state. The KFC Yum! Center in downtown Louisville can host just over twenty-two thousand fans for home basketball games, and those fans have the opportunity to rock their red and white chicken bucket hats for the games! (Okay, not all do, but the opportunity is there if you so choose.)

The Wildcats kick off at Kroger Field, which also holds roughly sixty-one thousand fans. But it's the storied Rupp Arena that sets most of the attendance records. Although Syracuse may have the largest capacity arena on record for a collegiate basketball team, Rupp Arena and Kentucky fans are the NCAA men's basketball attendance leaders nearly every year. Officially, Rupp Arena has a 20,500 person capacity, but fans have set or broken the record twenty-four times since the venue opened. One of these—no surprise here—was Kentucky vs. Louisville in 2010, when they topped out at just under twenty-five thousand in attendance. Just for fun, we'll tell you that only fifteen towns in Kentucky have populations of more than twenty-five thousand. Just think about what it must feel like to stand on the court as a visiting team and look up to see that kind of crowd.

12 | FESTIVALS CELEBRATING KENTUCKY

I like to see a man proud of the place in which he lives.
I like to see a man live so that his place will be proud of him.

ABRAHAM LINCOLN

A small green sign on the side of the road just as you enter Campbellsville, Kentucky, welcomes you to the home of PGA professional golfer J. B. Holmes. On light posts lining the street along the riverwalk in Owensboro, you'll find flags celebrating famous faces from the town, Johnny Depp among them. On the sides of buildings scattered throughout Louisville there are black-and-white portraits, eight or more stories high, of the city's most recognizable faces, including Muhammad Ali, Diane Sawyer, and Jennifer Lawrence. Downtown Hodgenville, birthplace of President Abraham Lincoln, is built around a square with a statue of Honest Abe at its very center. A banner stretched across Main Street in Central City boasts that the Muhlenberg County town is the proud home of the Everly Brothers. Across Kentucky, the state shows its pride in its famous people and recognizes their achievements with enthusiasm.

Kentucky communities also boast about their success stories, historic events, and traditions. We want everyone who visits to understand our pride in our people and in our achievements.

Never is this celebration of culture, heritage, and tradition more apparent in the multitude of festivals that span all twelve months and every theme you could dream up. Owensboro hosts the Bluegrass Music Festival in celebration of Kentucky's native son Bill Monroe, the father of bluegrass music. Fulton hosts the Banana

Festival, a revelry that honors a quirky part of its history. At one time, it had the only ice house along the route of refrigerated train cars that transported produce, like bananas, from the southern ports north to the country's metropolitan areas—keeping those bananas from spoiling before they reached their destination. Ham Fest in Trigg County honors the region's long history with the pork industry with a pig calling contest and selection of a prize-winning country ham.

These festivals have the things you'd expect—food vendors hustling funnel cakes and other deep-fried delicacies, arts and crafts, a handful of carnival rides, face painters, live music, and never enough bathrooms—but those details come secondary. They enhance the event, but they're not the purpose for the festival.

Our favorite festivals celebrate all things Kentucky, with great music shows, a week of events to honor a former president, and one of the most delicious barbecue competitions you can dream up. And, hey, we have the world's largest stainless steel chicken fryer! These are some of our favorite Kentucky community traditions.

An Ode to Bluegrass and Other Music Festivals

The origins of bluegrass music can be traced back to Ireland, Scotland, and England. When settlers from these countries arrived in Kentucky, they brought with them styles of music that were the roots of modern bluegrass music. Their songs had a distinctive sound and told the stories of their daily life. Bluegrass blends elements of mountain music with gospel and blues.

Bill Monroe, a native of Rosine, Kentucky, is often called the Father of Bluegrass Music. He grew up working and playing music with his siblings on the family farm on Jerusalem Ridge in the early 1900s. We'll tell you more about Monroe in part six, but in December 1945, he took his mandolin to the Ryman Auditorium stage in Nashville and, joined by Earl Scruggs on banjo and Lester Flatt on guitar, created a new form of American music: bluegrass.

Now, Nashville claims to be the birthplace of bluegrass music, but how could that be when Monroe honed his craft in Kentucky? And he wasn't alone. Loretta Lynn grew up a "Coal Miner's Daughter" in Butcher Holler. Rosemary Clooney of Maysville made her name with a string of pop hits in the 1950s and was also an incredible jazz vocalist. The Kentucky talent goes on and on, and we have a diverse lineup of festivals to celebrate this great musical tradition.

R.O.M.P. (River of Music Party), Owensboro

Sponsored by the Bluegrass Music Hall of Fame and Museum, the River of Music Party, or R.O.M.P., is the perfect place to stomp your boots. Steve Martin, Emmylou Harris, Rhiannon Giddens, Robert Earl Keen, and other stars like the Punch Brothers and Patty Loveless have rocked the stage at R.O.M.P. Fest over the past twenty years. Attendees are welcome to camp out for the shows in Yellow Creek Park and are also welcome to bring along their own instruments to jam through a full weekend of music workshops, art and food vendors, clogging, yoga, and children's entertainment. While you're in Daviess County for the festival, you can visit the Bluegrass Music Hall of Fame and Museum right down the road to pay homage to Bill Monroe, the Carter Family, J. D. Crowe, Hazel Dickens, and Alice Gerrard, among other legends of the genre.

Festival of the Bluegrass, Lexington

Also of note is the Festival of the Bluegrass at the Kentucky Horse Park in Lexington, where over the years Ricky Skaggs, Béla Fleck, and a teenage Alison Krauss have wowed fans in Central Kentucky. Bill Monroe and Ralph Stanley were among the festival's original entertainment when it began in 1974.

Forecastle Festival, Louisville

In the Louisville area, Forecastle Festival has been rocking since 2002 with acts from local favorites like My Morning Jacket, Sturgill Simpson, and Cage the Elephant, and national artists like Wilco, Arcade Fire, and Jack White. It has an international attendance, but Forecastle doesn't ignore its Kentucky roots. At the festival, the Kentucky Distillers Association and the Bourbon Trail host the Bourbon Lodge, featuring tastings, lessons with distillers and mixologists, and meals with bourbon pairings. And the charitable Forecastle Foundation gives back to the state by its support of the Kentucky Natural Lands Trust and other environmental nonprofits.

Railbird Festival, Lexington
A railbird is a horse racing enthusiast who sticks close to the action, hanging on the rail, if you will. Railbird Festival was originally hosted at Keeneland Race Track in Lexington for a weekend in August; now the two-day music festival is held at Lexington's Red Mile. The venue has three stages that feature national and local acts, and it offers unique bourbon and culinary experiences.

Appalshop, Whitesburg
In Whitesburg, in Letcher County, Appalshop hosts the Seedtime on the Cumberland Festival. Originally founded in 1969 as the Appalachian Film Workshop, this nonprofit hosts a radio and television station, oral history and film archive, theater and art productions, and community development projects among many other good works. The Seedtime on the Cumberland Festival is their annual celebration of regional musicians; it also showcases Appalachian artists, writers, and crafts. Seedtime on the Cumberland is unique in that it provides a platform for mountain music of all genres, from bluegrass to punk.

Lincoln Days

Abraham Lincoln, the sixteenth president of the United States, was born February 12, 1809, in a simple log cabin on a farm near Hodgen's Mill in LaRue County, Kentucky. You can visit that log cabin in Hodgenville today to see just how humble Lincoln's beginnings were. (The entire cabin might fit inside your bedroom, perhaps even your bathroom.) With little formal education, Lincoln went on to become an attorney, an accomplished politician and moral leader, and a great statesman known worldwide. He led the nation through a civil war and issued the Emancipation Proclamation, which was the beginning to the end of slavery in the United States.

Lincoln won political office in Illinois, but he was always a proud Kentuckian. He once said, "I like to see a man proud of the place in which he lives. I like to see a man live so that his place will be proud of him." The citizens of LaRue County show their pride in him each October at the Lincoln Days celebration. The two-day festival honors Abraham Lincoln's legacy and promotes the town's cultural and civic interests, with a little fun thrown in too. You can enter for your chance to win the Abraham and Mary Todd Lincoln look-alike contest, and stick around for great food and local crafts.

Favorite Food Festivals

By now, you're well-versed in how to eat like a Kentuckian, so you know just how much our food means to us. Many Kentucky culinary traditions are rooted in a history of necessity, born of the circumstances of the times. Our family recipes and our cultural dishes are ingrained in us—burgoo was a product of the need to feed large families with whatever game could be hunted; we barbecue mutton because western Kentucky was once a big sheep farming region; we started adding oats to our sausage to stretch the meat farther; the first Hot Brown was stacked because hungry partygoers would accept no excuse from a chef who ran low on ingredients. We know these stories as well as we know our grandmothers' recipes for transparent pie (if they'll even tell you the correct recipe), and they're important to the communities that raised us.

Our food festivals span the entire calendar year, and they celebrate the things you may expect: fried chicken, beer cheese, burgoo, and barbecue. But we also have annual bashes in honor of bananas, pecans, mushrooms, and apples. These aren't just the flavor of the week—all these foods have had an impact on the Commonwealth's storied history. And each dish is more delicious than the last. If you want to learn more about these iconic Kentucky foods, head back to part one.

- World Chicken Festival, London (September)
- Spoonbread Festival, Berea (September)
- Banana Festival, Fulton (September)
- Mountain Mushroom Festival, Irvine (April)

Enjoying food, sharing stories, and spending time in the kitchen together is at the heart of being a Kentuckian. We honor history and tradition and pass it on no matter how quirky, even as we continue to innovate. You might say we could write a whole book about it—wait, we did! If you want to learn more about the Commonwealth's greatest cuisine, check out our *Famous Kentucky Flavors*.

Kentucky Bucket List

We love a reason to celebrate. Here are a few things to add to that ever-growing list to make sure you're getting the full experience. We have so many great traditions to honor, don't miss a single one!

1. We love the Derby, but go to the Oaks or Thurby. After you attend one Kentucky Derby, shift gears and go to the Kentucky Oaks on the Friday before. Or if you're local, give Thurby a try. Less crowded, less insane, these races earlier in Derby week can be just as glamorous as the Derby if you want them to be. The other great thing? They can also be casual. If you don't feel like getting all decked out, that's okay!

2. Welcome teams home with fanfare. Even with two teams that win a lot of games and tournament titles, it never gets old welcoming them back home to hang a championship banner. Kentucky fans like to meet their team at Bluegrass Airport in Lexington when they taxi into the terminal. They bring their homemade, congratulatory signs to stand outside the runway fences and make sure the team hears the roar of their love. In Louisville, community restaurants and bars have even been known to hang replica championship banners from their rooftops to support the team during the season.

3. Catch the best fireworks show ever. Thunder Over Louisville is free, and there are food vendors, merch, and other fairway-style rides and games. The best place to catch all the festivities is Waterfront Park on River Road. But, if you're not a fan of crowds, you can watch the fireworks for free from plenty of public places along the river. Ticketed watch parties are hosted by radio stations, the Louisville Bats baseball team, and the KFC Yum! Center and are held at local venues such as the Galt House, the Belle of Louisville riverboat, and restaurants along the river.

4. Sit on the bluegrass and enjoy some Bluegrass. Get your blanket ready and stretch out across that bright green Kentucky bluegrass for good food, time with friends, and some quality banjo-picking. Owensboro has R.O.M.P., Lexington has the Festival of the Bluegrass, and bluegrass music is played at many other community events throughout the year.

5. Grab breakfast at the track. A favorite Kentucky tradition is to enjoy breakfast trackside at Keeneland in Lexington. The Keeneland Track Kitchen is a well-kept secret, but one we'll happily share with you. One of the best breakfasts in Kentucky (and that's saying a lot!), it opens at 6 a.m. each morning, except for major holidays. You don't have to be a horseman to enjoy their home-style food, but you just might find yourself seated next to a famous trainer or jockey! Grab breakfast and then walk along the track to watch morning workouts. Horses train even when the meets aren't running.

Suggested Reading

To learn more about the Bluegrass State's festivals and traditions, our college sports, our historic horse races, our culinary histories, and our great music, here is a suggested reading list.

Bolin, James Duane. *Adolph Rupp and the Rise of Kentucky Basketball.* Lexington: University Press of Kentucky, 2020.

Cox, Joe, and Ryan Clark. *Fightin' Words: Kentucky vs. Louisville.* New York: Skyhorse, 2016.

Hall, Joe B. *Coach Hall: My Life On and Off the Court.* Lexington: University Press of Kentucky, 2019.

Howard, Jason. *A Few Honest Words: The Kentucky Roots of Popular Music.* Lexington: University Press of Kentucky, 2015.

Louie B. Nunn Center for Oral History. https: //www.kentucky oralhistory.org/.

McDaniels, Pellom, III. *The Prince of Jockeys: The Life of Isaac Burns Murphy.* Lexington: University Press of Kentucky, 2018.

Nicholson, James C. *The Kentucky Derby: How the Run for the Roses Became America's Premier Sporting Event.* Lexington: University Press of Kentucky, 2014.

Smith, Gerald L., Karen Cotton McDaniel, and John A. Hardin, eds. *The Kentucky African American Encyclopedia.* Lexington: University Press of Kentucky, 2015.

Stevens, Peggy Noe, and Susan Reigler. *Which Fork Do I Use with My Bourbon?: Setting the Table for Tastings, Food Pairings, Dinners, and Cocktail Parties.* Lexington: University Press of Kentucky, 2020.

Thompson, Hunter S. "The Kentucky Derby Is Decadent and Depraved, " Grantland. May 13, 2013. http://grantland.com /features/looking-back-hunter-s-thompson-classic-story -kentucky-derby/.

Wolfe, Charles K. *Kentucky Country: Folk and Country Music of Kentucky.* Lexington: University Press of Kentucky, 1996.

PART 5
GONNA TALK REAL SLOW FOR Y'ALL

To be born in Kentucky is a heritage; to brag
about it is a habit; to appreciate it is a virtue.

IRVIN S. COBB

If your accent is part of your vocal personality, then it's no
surprise that the Kentucky accent is diverse and interesting.
With roots in the Elizabethan English of the state's earliest settlers,
it has been influenced by others over the years: southerners, Native
Americans, and, with the urbanization that followed the Civil War,
northerners. As you travel across the Commonwealth from east
to west, you hear the accent (and the dialect) change.

Kentuckians pronounce our eastern mountain region "App-
ah-*latch*-uh," not "App-ah-*lay*-shuh." We say "Luhl-vuhl," not
"Looey-ville." In general, any time a Kentucky town name ends
in "ville," you're going to want to pronounce it "vuhl." And while
we're at it, "Ver-sigh" is in France, but "Ver-sales" is in Kentucky.

One of our fathers tells a story about being introduced to new
fraternity brothers during recruitment back in the early 1970s. He
found it a little odd that there were quite so many "Mac's" in this
particular house. Being from Louisville, Dad hadn't yet picked up
that his new fraternity brother, from near Pikeville, was introduc-
ing him to a lot of "Mikes."

Over time, accents can disappear. As communities evolve and
families move, the sounds of Kentucky change with them. But
much like the fierceness with which Kentuckians protect their
histories, traditions, and ways of life, they also protect the way they

talk. We're proud of our accents, our turns of phrase, our breaking vowels, and our "maters" and "taters." You'll pick it up in no time. There's more to know about where those sounds came from and the importance of how accents are a big part of our identity.

13 | THE ACCENT

"Where exactly are you from?" It's a question many Kentuckians get, whether they're traveling north into Yankee territory or south into Dixie, because our accents are, well, just different. Not quite northern, not quite midwestern. Somewhat resemblant of the famous southern drawl, and in the eastern part of the state, distinctly Appalachian.

If you travel across Kentucky from one side to the other, you'll see changes in geography, in culture, in traditions, and in accents. In the east, the Appalachian accent has the distinctive sounds of Elizabethan English. In the Bluegrass region, the influence of slavery, followed by urbanization, resulted in some people having a southern accent and others, a "neutral" accent. The western Kentucky accent, with its twang, is a different version of the southern sound.

Language is fascinating: the way we say words and why, the turns of phrase that certain regions have adopted that you don't hear anywhere else. Accents are passed down in families like hair color and the nose shape. And while they fade as we move to larger cities or move across state and regional lines, the history and culture associated with their distinctive sounds live on.

Where Does the Kentucky Accent Come From?

It's not really possible to divide Kentucky into just three regions: "east, central, and west," or "right, middle, and left." But when considering accents, three or four varieties are predominant.

In the mountains in Eastern Kentucky, you'll find communities speaking Appalachian English. Some say this dialect is one of the oldest varieties of English spoken in the country, with linguistic elements found in Shakespearean and Elizabethan English. There are similarities: words like "afeared," "airish," and "brickle," all Shakespearean, have been forgotten by most English speakers outside of Appalachia. And Appalachians say "might could" instead of "may be able to," add "'un" to the end of words as in "young'un," and use "done" as a helping verb—"He's done finished it." These turns of phrase were common in England in the seventeenth and eighteenth centuries.

The Appalachian accent and dialect is derived from the earliest settlers to this region. Unusual for Kentucky, it doesn't show Native American influence (although "Appalachia" is a Native American word). The Appalachian accent is one of the toughest to lose, whether because of its distinctiveness or the stubbornness of those proud to be born and raised there.

Around the turn of the eighteenth century, Appalachian explorers, including Kentucky's James Bowie along with Stephen F. Austin, Sam Houston, and Davy Crockett, helped found the Republic of Texas. Perhaps their strong Appalachian roots explain why elements of Appalachian English are heard in parts of Texas (for instance, saying "we liketa" to mean "we nearly"), despite the states being more than twelve hundred miles apart.

So, what makes up this distinctive Eastern Kentucky sound? The "ah" vowel sound replaces the long "i" vowel sound in most instances: "wire" is pronounced "war"; "fire" is "far"; and "retire" is "retar." Words may be shortened and altered, with an "-er" replacing a long "o" at the end. So "potato" becomes "tader"; "tomato" becomes "mader"; and "tobacco" becomes "backer."

Accents in central Kentucky's Bluegrass region are split, either a traditional southern drawl or neutral. The area is home to the state's two largest cities—Louisville and Lexington. As Kentuckians move to the big city, and as people not born in the Bluegrass move to the state, many regional dialects have been abandoned. Additionally, mainstream media and sources of entertainment are increasingly accent-neutral; kids mimic what they hear on their screens and lose their accent.

The sounds that do linger in this region are reminiscent of Older Southern American English. We don't have the classic "magnolia drawl" with its impossibly long syllables and broken vowels, but we show other distinctive aspects of the southern accent and use grammatical innovations such as "y'all" and "fixin' to." It's part of the same shift that makes us lose our distinctive dialect—rural southerners move to cities and mix all of the different rural varieties together into a more uniform sound.

Like the accent of a New Yorker or a Bostonian, only in a totally different way, the Kentucky accent that comes from Older Southern American English is non-rhotic, or in other words, it drops the "r." Similar to Appalachian English, this Kentucky southern accent also replaces the long "i" sound with "ah." So "eye" is more like "ahh" and "my" like "mah." You don't "buy" something at the store, you "bah" it. Additionally, "get" does not rhyme with "yet" in Kentucky. It is pronounced "git." We can't speak for all Kentucky mothers, but growing up ours had a saying that went like this: "You get what you get, so don't throw a fit." Because "get" rhymes with "fit." A friend from outside of Kentucky once told us that they had heard another version of that same saying: "You get what you get, so don't be upset." Strange, that doesn't rhyme at all!

Other distinctions include extending the short "a" or "schwa" vowel sounds into long "a" or "ai" sounds. "Can't" rhymes with "paint."

In western Kentucky, the accent takes on a twang, like the words have been rolling across the state from east to west. It is similar to the Kentucky southern drawl, but is more nasal and a bit sharper. Syllables are added whenever possible. "There" is pronounced "they-yur" and "bed" is "bay-ehd." This twang also puts the emphasis on the first syllable. You're watching "TEE-vee," don't forget your "UHM-brella," don't step in wet "CEE-ment," and look out for the "PO-leese."

Suggested Reading

Our discussion of Kentucky dialects and accents has barely scratched the surface. For a deeper dive, here is our suggested reading list.

Appalshop, https://appalshop.org/.

Clark, Amy D., and Nancy M. Hayward, eds. *Talking Appalachian: Voice, Identity, and Community.* Lexington: University Press of Kentucky, 2014.

Dictionary of American Regional English (DARE). https://www-daredictionary-com.

"How Y'all, Youse and You Guys Talk," dialect quiz from the *New York Times*, 2013. https: //www.nytimes.com/interactive /2014/upshot/dialect-quiz-map.html.

Jones, Loyal. *Appalachian Values.* Ashland: Jesse Stuart Foundation, 1975.

Loyal Jones Appalachian Center at Berea College. https: //www .berea.edu/appalachian-center/.

Rennick, Robert M. *Kentucky Place Names.* Lexington: University Press of Kentucky, 1988.

Shackelford, Laurel, and Bill Weinberg. *Our Appalachia: An Oral History.* Lexington: University Press of Kentucky, 1988.

14 | HOW DOES THAT TRANSLATE?

Sometimes it is more than the Kentucky accent that gives an outsider pause when they find themselves knee-deep in a story being told by one of the men camped out on a bench in front of the courthouse. They may understand all of the words and what each word means individually, but not necessarily follow once those words are all strung together.

Just take one of our favorite Kentucky sayings, "Rode hard and put up wet." Um. OK? If we say that about someone, we're saying they look tired, mentally and/or physically haggard, totally worn out. So why couldn't we just say *that*? Well, the phrase originates in horse racing, so it isn't surprising that it is a Kentucky favorite. When horses are practicing or running a race, they develop a lather of foamy sweat on the outside of their coat. If you ride a horse hard and then put him up in the stable without being washed, dried off, and groomed, he gets very uncomfortable and agitated. Not to mention, he'll look messy and dirty the next time you bring him out to saddle up. You have to make sure to let your horse cool down after a race.

Here's a beginner's guide to "speaking Kentucky" and to navigating some of our unusual place names. While the many phrases and words in this chapter aren't necessarily unique to Kentucky, they are often defined and used slightly differently in the Commonwealth.

A Few Favorite Kentucky Sayings

We won't claim that these are never used anywhere else, nor will we claim to have captured them all. But here are a few of our favorite Kentucky sayings with the necessary translations:

Fair to middling: This is a response to "How are you doing?" It basically means "OK, fair, so-so."

Have a goodin: A farewell, loosely translated to "Have a good day/night/weekend." Just, have a good one.

Ornery as a mule: Frequently used among spouses, but it can certainly be used in more diverse cases. In truth, mules (the product of a horse crossed with a donkey) are much smarter than they are stubborn, but we use the phrase to mean that someone is particularly stuck in their ways and unwilling to budge.

Meaner than a copper moccasin: Copperhead, water moccasin—honestly, we don't care which poisonous, fang-bearing snake we're talking about, so we often just combine 'em. This phrase originates in the assumption that poisonous snakes are mean and likely to lash out and cause serious damage. So, if we're referring to a person when using this phrase, we may not mean that they'll bite to kill, but watch your back.

Well, I'll be: Commonly used to express surprise.

Rode hard and put up wet: With origins in horse racing, this phrase means you look tired or physically and/or mentally exhausted and haggard.

Bless your heart: Usually uttered by a woman (quite often one of our mothers) when expressing concern—sometimes genuine, sometimes slightly less than genuine—or pity. It may be used in place of "you poor thing," and it may be delivered with a hint of sarcasm. It is often accompanied by a general clutching of the pearls or a hand over the heart gesture.

Full as a tick on a coon dog's back: Totally and completely full after a meal. Stuffed.

Were you raised in a barn?: Typically said instead of telling you to close the door. Don't let all that bought air out.

Praise the Lord and pass the gravy: One of our most favorite and brief blessings said before a meal.

Good Lord willing and the creek don't rise: Basically, if the Lord wants me to, I'll do it. More literally: if God so wills me to do something and as long as heavy rains do not wash away bridges or parts of dirt roads so that I can safely travel to carry out this endeavor.

What in tarnation?: An expression of surprise or bewilderment. Tarnation comes from the word "darnation," which was an adaptation of "damnation" and was used in more polite conversation.

A month of Sundays: A very long time. Usually used by a grandparent to express how long it has been since you've been by to see them.

Champing at the bit: As in, ready to go, can't wait to get started, or sometimes an impatient response to being restrained. This originates in the horse racing industry. When horses are ready to race, they champ repeatedly and restlessly on the bit in their mouths, which is connected to the reins, signaling to their rider that they want to run. Sometimes this phrase is incorrectly said "chomping at the bit," but the sentiment is the same. Some of our other favorite phrases that have horse-racing origins include "hands down," which means an easy victory or without contest. The saying comes from the way jockeys lower their hands to slacken the reins in order to ease up their mounts when securing an easy victory. Another favorite is "in the home stretch" or "in the home straight," which is used when people are nearing the end or the final stage of something. This refers to the final part of the horse race after the final turn when the horses race down the straight of the horse track to the finish line.

Some Things Mean Something Different in Kentucky

Here's a helpful guide to some of the words and gestures you'll hear across the Bluegrass State that might means something slightly different than they do other places:

The one-finger wave: No, not *that* finger. Gosh, y'all. This is the index finger, sometimes we call it the pointer finger, wave that you do when two hands are on the steering wheel, and you pass an on-coming car on a country road. It's our friendly way of saying "hi, y'all," but safely, of course.

Coke: The universal word used for any soft drink. In parts of southeastern Kentucky, you'll sometimes hear it called "pop."

Y'all: A far superior way to say "you all." Often used in friendly salutations. Often overused by these two Kentuckians.

Toboggan: A warm winter hat. Not a sled.

Court Days: Not requiring a call to your lawyer, Court Days refers to a community festival or gathering day.

Buggy: You might be thinking of the horse-drawn kind, but this is what we call a grocery cart.

Mom'n'ems: Your mother's house or anyone in your mother's family and/or friends circle. We say this when we're going to visit our mom's house or anyone's house in that related group.

Reckon: Guess, figure. As in, "I reckon' we'll head on to Mom'n'ems."

All git-out: As in "all get-out," for when you want to express something is amazing. He can play guitar like all git-out!

Supper: Another word for dinner, this is what we call the last meal of the day (not counting that midnight snack, of course).

Highfalutin: Fine, fancy, superior. Usually used when we're talking about people who are trying to impose a fancy way of doing something or those who are sharing their thoughts in a pompous tone.

Fixin': Getting ready to do something.

Spell: A frame of time, usually to rest, like, "I need a breathin' spell." It can also be used as a verb for "relieve" or "stand in for." You might ask a friend, "Can you spell me while I take a quick break?"

Stories: While primarily used by our grandmothers to describe their daytime shows such as soap operas, stories can be used to describe any television program that you're fixin' to catch up on.

Warsh: It's how we pronounce "wash." As a noun, the laundry. Count your blessings if your granny doesn't still use a clothesline.

Young'uns: Children or anyone younger than the person calling them a young'un.

Do what?: Always said in a conversation after someone tells you something, usually when you didn't quite hear them, but sometimes even if you did.

Used to could: Something you used to be able to do but now can't. Usually when referring to that state championship your football, basketball, baseball, etc., team won sometime five-plus decades ago.

Kentucky Place Names

The names of cities and towns get reused and recycled across the country and the world. While some cities have names so distinctive, they rarely need a state clarification—such as Los Angeles, Chicago, New York, Houston, and Orlando—others could be confused with towns of the same name in locations across the globe. In Kentucky, we have our fair share of famous and, well, unique place names. Here are a few of our favorites:

- Possum Trot is a dot on the map in Marshall County, east of Paducah. To the west of that western town, you'll find Monkeys Eyebrow. Note that it is not the possessive "monkey's, " and while it never had a post office and so can't technically be called a town, don't ever say that to the locals.
- There are ten different towns named Mud Lick in Kentucky. You can find them in Anderson, Elliott, Greenup, Knox, Lewis, Monroe, Perry, Pike, Robertson, and Russell Counties. This should not be confused with Paint Lick in Garrard County.
- Future City in Ballard County got its name from the developer who put up a sign at the edge of the land where he intended to build a town that said, "Future City." And then he never got around to changing it.
- Bush in Laurel County was named after George Bush, but not either one of the presidents by that name. This George Bush founded the town in 1840 when he opened the post office and general store. The first President George Bush campaigned there in 1988. The newspaper headline read "Bush Returns to Bush."
- Other favorites include Black Gnat in Taylor County, Black Snake in Bell County, Co-operative in McCreary County, Crummies in Harlan County, Hi Hat in Floyd County, Paradise in Muhlenberg County (of the famed John Prime song, "Paradise"), Quality in Butler County, Subtle in Metcalf County, Susie in Wayne County, Whoopee in Ohio County, Yosemite (pronounced "yahss-uh-might") in Casey County, and Wild Cat in Clay County.

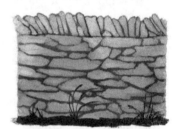

The Grass Is Actually Green, Most of the Time

It is a common misconception of non-native Kentuckians that as soon as they cross the state line, those rolling acres of bright green grass are going to turn blue. While it seems like a silly notion, to be fair, Kentucky has declared itself The Bluegrass State, and at least half of us claim to "bleed blue" (in reference to being Kentucky Wildcats fans). But the grass in Kentucky is actually just regular green grass. So, what gives?

Bluegrass, or *Poa pratensis*, is a type of grass seed that is incredibly common in North America and is found in many places outside of Kentucky. Contrary to some accounts, it isn't Kentucky's famous limestone that gives the grass a hint of azure, anil, or topaz (although it does wonders for our bourbon). And it isn't named for its leaves, which stay green year-round. The grass is named for its seed heads, which appear during the spring and summer when the grass is allowed to grow unshorn to a natural height of one to three feet. An unmowed field of seeding *Poa pratensis* waving in a summer breeze is undeniably blue in color. Rolling expanses of untouched fields shining in the morning dew give the state its moniker, the Bluegrass State.

15 | TALK SPORTS WITH THE BEST OF THEM

As you'll have gathered by now, in Kentucky, sports are a big deal. Basketball isn't a game, it's a way of life and, for many, it's a religion. Saturdays in the fall are reserved for all-day tailgating and cheering on your favorite school against an in-state rival's football team. And the first Saturday in May isn't just the fastest two minutes in sports, it is a day like no other in the Bluegrass. Our teams and our Thoroughbreds make us proud, and we are their biggest fans and their harshest—but most supportive—critics. Our kids, whether they bleed red or blue, can recite national championship years, know how many games it takes to be bowl game eligible, and can school you on the ins and outs of a racing form. We teach them well.

Root, Root, Root for Your Home Team

College sports run deep in many Kentucky families, and the Friday night dinner table will often include discussion about who is likely to start in tomorrow night's game. Or you can call in to a talk radio show on the topic ("First time caller, long-time fan, y'all"). There are many great state schools to cheer for, but in most Kentucky communities you're either a Louisville fan or you "bleed blue."

You can't go wrong cheering for the teams of either of these great schools, both have an impressive history (see part four), but at some point you're probably going to be asked: Cards or Cats?

One of the most identifiable markers of an athletics team is its mascot. The first person known to have donned the University of Louisville Cardinal costume was T. Lee Adams in 1953. His cloth outfit was created by Frances Goldsmith, a faculty member in the home economics department. The mascot was initially just known as the "Cardinal Bird," but around 2012, the Louisville athletics program named him "Louie." One interesting distinction about Louie the Cardinal? He has teeth. While real cardinals don't have teeth, obviously, his mouth of pearly whites does give Louie a threatening look that indicates a strong fighting spirit.

If you're at a UofL game, get your "L's" ready. The members of Louisville's 1988 basketball signing class say they invented the "L's Up" hand signal: make the letter L with your thumb, index, and middle fingers and hold it above your head while shouting, "Go Cards!"

If you "bleed blue" or are a member of BBN (Big Blue Nation), you're a University of Kentucky Wildcat. The "Wildcats" nickname became synonymous with UK shortly after a 6–2 football victory over Illinois on the road on October 9, 1909 (it was noted that the team "fought like wildcats"). The mascot itself appeared in 1976, with Gary Tanner as the original Wildcat. A few years later he was joined by another cat that walked on stilts, during the "twin tower" era of basketball players Melvin Turpin and Sam Bowie. Today, the Wildcat is joined by Scratch, a mascot known for his comedy antics.

At basketball games, students stand in the eRUPPtion Zone. They sing the lyrics of the school fight song that they know by heart, and at the end of each game—win or lose—they stick around to sing "My Old Kentucky Home" together. It's nearly as moving as hearing the state song sung at the Derby.

OK, But Have You Heard the Bear Bryant Cadillac Story?

Let it be known that Kentuckians love a good story. Give us a rumor, spin us a tall tale—we'll be eating out of your hands. A good juicy combination of all the above that involves two of the state's most famous college athletic coaches? Well, we're as happy as a dead pig laying in the sunshine. You have our full attention. Today, Kentucky has some of the most famous college sports teams in the country, but just talk to your resident season ticket holders, and they'll bend your ear about the good ole days. For instance, when Bear Bryant—yes, he is better known for his one million titles won at the University of Alabama, but hush now, we're telling this story—was coaching the University of Kentucky football team and legend Adolph Rupp was at the helm of the UK men's basketball team.

The University of Kentucky hired Paul "Bear" Bryant from the University of Maryland as its head football coach in 1946. He went on to lead the Wildcats to eight consecutive winning seasons, four bowl games, and its first SEC championship in 1950. In the Sugar Bowl that same year, Kentucky had a big win over national champion Oklahoma, breaking the team's thirty-one-game winning streak record and claiming the first (and at the time of this writing, only) football championship for UK. A few weeks before that big game, Bryant was quoted in an Associated Press article saying, "The other night we had a joint basketball-football banquet and Adolph Rupp was presented with a big four-door Cadillac. All I got was a cigarette lighter."

What was this all about? At the time, although he had a great record at UK, Bear Bryant wasn't the powerhouse coach that we know him as today, and basketball reigned supreme in the Bluegrass. Still, the fact that Rupp would get a snazzy car and Bryant would get a mere lighter, well, that's downright insulting. Bryant did stay on as head football coach for another three years, but he left Kentucky after the 1953 season for a position at Texas A&M. What made the coach leave? Many pointed to that whole Cadillac thing and blamed Rupp for the great football coach's departure.

Bryant's UK record of 60–23–5 stood for almost seventy years until Coach Mark Stoops broke it during the 2022 season.

It makes for a good story to pit the two great coaches against each other, but really each one was always supportive of the other. In fact, many think Bryant just made the whole thing up in good fun—you know, a joke. The local Lexington newspaper, the *Herald*, reported that Bryant made the remarks about his cigarette lighter in a light vein. Turns out, he was kidding. Telling a story. Spinning a yarn. Yanking their tails. You know, like Kentuckians generally enjoy doing.

There was actually a car in the mix—sort of. In 1946, just shortly after Bryant was hired at Kentucky, the Lexington Junior Chamber of Commerce held a reception at the Lexington Lafayette Hotel to celebrate Rupp and the 1946 NIT Championship season. At the banquet, the group awarded Rupp a certificate for an Oldsmobile sedan, but not the car itself. At the time, car factories had been converted to manufacture armaments for World War II. It wasn't until fall 1945 that automobile production resumed.

How to Place a Bet at the Racetrack

Whether you're dropping by the track on a normal day during a spring or fall meet, betting on a horse race at an out-of-state racetrack, or sipping on a mint julep at the Kentucky Derby, you're going to need to know what to say when you place your bet. This step-by-step advice will have you sounding like a seasoned pro at the window.

First things first, how do you pick a horse? Get your racing program and look at the fine print.

> **Stall/Gate Position:** Most horses begin from stalls, and some positions can have an impact on certain races. In general, remember that a sprint race will favor an outside stall and a longer race will favor an inside stall position.

How Long Since It Last Raced: You want the horse to be rested, but not too rested. Generally, the sweet spot of time between races is 30–60 days.

Finishing Place from Previous Races: Not the most reliable way to pick a horse, but you can look for patterns here. See if he places the same way more than once in a row. See if he's on a winning streak. But remember, many factors can influence how a horse finishes.

Distances Run vs. Course Wins: It doesn't just matter that the horse ran, how far was it running? There's a code for this in your racing form. A "C" next to the horse's name means the horse has previously won on the same course you're betting at. A "D" means the horse has won at the same distance it is racing that day. A "C" and a "D" together means the horse has run this same race before.

Jockey and Trainer Data: Not as big of a deal, but good to note if a particularly great trainer and/or jockey is partnered with the horse. Some Kentuckians have a favorite jockey or trainer, so any race they're involved in is an automatic bet.

Official Ranking: This is how each horse is ranked according to experts. Just remember, horses are animals and experts can be wrong.

If you're at the race track, don't forget to take a look at your horse. It seems sort of obvious, but you can tell a lot from looking at a horse. A friend once told us he always bet on the horse that, erm, used the bathroom while on the paddock just before a race. He took it as a good sign. We tend to look more at how the horse is acting. Is he tired or agitated? Does he look healthy and strong? Just like us, horses are affected by moods and sicknesses and other factors.

Finally, don't discount picking a horse based on a good name. You like the name Lucky Penny? Maybe she is one. Put your money on her.

Actually placing the bet is quite simple, but make sure you get the wording right so you know you're putting your money where you mean to, and so you sound like you know what you're talking about.

1. State the track name.
2. Say the race number.
3. Say the amount of money you want to wager.
4. State what type of wager you're making (win, place, show, etc.)
5. Say the horse number.

Example: "Keeneland. Race 4. $2 to win on #7."
To make sure you know what type of wager you want to make, here is a little bit more information:

To Win: You win if your horse finishes in first place.

To Place: You win if your horse finishes in first place or in second place.

To Show: You win if your horse finishes in first place, in second place, or in third place. As the odds increase, your winnings decrease. So, if you place the safe bet, to show, you have greater odds of winning, but you'll take home less money.

Exacta: Bet the horses to finish in first and second place. You win if they come in that exact order.

Trifecta: Bet the horses to finish in first, second, and third. You win if they come in that exact order.

Superfecta: Bet the horses to finish first, second, third, and fourth. You win if they come in that exact order.

A quick pro tip! You can "box" an exacta, trifecta, or superfecta bet. You'll pay more money for the bet, but the horses you pick can come in any order for you to be in the money. For example, you might bet an exacta box on horse 3 and 7. Your horses can *either* win or place for you to call your ticket a winner.

Kentucky Bucket List

Add these few things to your ever-growing Kentucky Bucket List. Y'all won't regret a trip to the track, a stop in Appalachia, or a road trip through some of our favorite Kentucky communities.

1. Place a bet at Keeneland or Churchill Downs. Pick out the best-named horse in the program, put $2 to win, and cross your fingers as you cheer him down the straight. There is nothing more exciting than picking the horse that wins the race, even when the payout is just a few bucks. And if the payout is a big one? Well, now that's a very good day.

2. Visit the Appalachian Artisan Center in Hindman. This center works to develop the economy of Eastern Kentucky through arts, culture, and heritage, and it provides assistance to artists, including business plan development, training, studio space, and exhibit opportunities. Visit the museum to learn more about the history and culture of Eastern Kentucky and to view some of the amazing original work from Appalachian artists.

3. Watch or listen to the recordings from Appalshop in Whitesburg. More than fifty years ago, Appalshop, a project of Lyndon B. Johnson's War on Poverty, started as a film workshop to document the people, businesses, environment, and history of the region. Since its founding, Appalshop has become a bastion of the arts in Eastern Kentucky; in addition to films, it produces music and oral history recordings, theater, and photography, and it runs the FM station WMMT, Mountain Community Radio. Appalshop maintains an archive of their work, which can be purchased and streamed at their website. May we recommend *Mud Creek*

Clinic, a film about Eula Hall, known as the Mother of the Mountains, and the founding of the clinic that to this day continues to help the underserved communities around Floyd County, Kentucky.

4. Drive through Horse Country in the Bluegrass on a dewy morning. On a foggy, dewy morning in late spring, a drive through the rolling hills of Horse Country in the Bluegrass region will give you a glimpse of the blue color that made Kentucky's grass famously blue. It'll be growing tall and seeding, and in that early morning light, you'll see fields of blue. What a wonderful world.

5. Attend the annual Tobacco Cutting Contest in Garrard County. Tobacco is an extremely labor-intensive crop. At the end of the summer, tobacco farmers and any help they can find must move through their fields and hand cut the tobacco leaves row by row. Then they hang it in barns to cure. Since 1981, to honor the state's cash crop tradition, the Garrard County Cooperative Extension Service has hosted an annual contest to see who can cut it the fastest. The community comes out to watch farmers compete in a battle against time and the elements—it is always brutally hot. It's an impressive sight, and you might just learn what the exact measurements are for a bushel, a peck, or, because it is Kentucky, a shit ton.

6. Take a road trip to Rabbit Hash, Bugtussle, Paradise, Versailles, or another town that is uniquely Kentucky. There's always something to discover in a small Kentucky town. In Rabbit Hash, visit the General Store. The historic site burned to the ground a few years ago but has since been restored. In Versailles, stay in a real castle. The views are amazing. Say hello to a fellow Kentuckian for us. Everyone has a great story to tell.

PART 6
A STORY OF GREAT KENTUCKIANS

I hope to have God on my side, but I must have Kentucky.

ABRAHAM LINCOLN

When folks think of great intellectuals, writers, scientists, artists, and musicians, they may think of professors in ivory towers on the East Coast, or of the well-known names seen in museums in Washington, DC, and New York, or printed on *New York Times* bestsellers and on iconic album covers. Kentucky is, perhaps, a forgotten powerhouse of great thought, art, music, and letters. After all, our state claims the first university established west of the Allegheny Mountains (Transylvania, in Lexington), not one, but *two* Nobel Prizes for genetics, and more than our fair share of Pulitzer Prizes and bestselling writers.

Our giftedness comes from several sources. For one, we were formed by the creative spirit of our foremothers who crossed the Appalachian Mountains to build a new life in an unknown land. And Kentucky, at the crossroads of eight other states, receives a mix of influences that spark creativity in us and our communities. Perhaps we are driven by the spirit of hard work and our sense of pride in where we come from—and the desire for that place to be proud of us right back.

Long gone are the stereotypes that would picture a Kentuckian as a country bumpkin with no shoes (and/or teeth). We may dress in jeans and boots or in a three-piece suit; we may report from the White House or write from the silence of a convent—long live the genius of the Bluegrass State.

As the two of us grew up in Kentucky, the music, art, and literature were just as important and formative in our education and personhood as anything else on the school's curriculum. Fortunately, we had teachers, family, and communities that praised the value of the arts and humanities and embedded that reverence in our minds. Our hope is that the young people of Kentucky today have the opportunity to learn and to grow from the bright sparks that came before. That our governments and school systems will continue to fund the arts and humanities, recognizing the value of a well-rounded education for future Kentuckians.

16 | ROOTED IN KENTUCKY

THE STATE'S FAMOUS WRITERS

Until the last fifty years or so, growing up on a tobacco farm was a common experience for young folks in Kentucky. Perhaps the solitude and the time for meditation that are part of working on the farm helped shape one of the state's greatest thinkers—our Kentucky version of Henry David Thoreau. Is Wendell Berry a poet who is also a farmer? Or a farmer who is also a poet? It's hard to separate Berry's writing from his agrarian roots and his ecological activism.

Berry was born and raised in Henry County, Kentucky, near Port Royal, and he still lives there. His long legacy includes influential works of fiction (like *Nathan Coulter* and *Jayber Crow*), nonfiction (like *The Unsettling of America* and *Sex, Economy, Freedom, and Community*), and poetry (like *The Country of Marriage* and *The Farm*) along with internationally renowned awards including the National Humanities Medal.

Berry left the farm to attend the University of Kentucky, where he received his bachelor's and master's degrees; later, he attended Stanford University as a Wallace Stegner Fellow. His studies in creative writing nurtured his development as a writer, inside and outside of the classroom. He was influenced by a literary community that included fellow Kentuckians Gurney Norman, James Baker Hall, and Ed McClanahan, and in the 1960s, by young American writers who converged in California's Bay Area, including Ken Kesey, Larry McMurtry, and Ernest Gaines.

Wendell Berry's career proves you don't need to flee to the big city to share big ideas. Following his Stegner Fellowship, he knocked around the world teaching for a few years and then brought his family back to Henry County in 1965. He bought the farm and homestead, where they still live off the land. This way of life crystallized much of the philosophical and ecological thinking that underpins his work. His fiction, nonfiction, essays, and poetry are all informed by a reliance on the soil and natural resources that has disappeared from much of modern society. Berry's themes of activism, sustainable agriculture, and the connection to place continue to ring through American life and influence other thinkers and writers.

A deep connection to place is not uniquely Kentuckian, but it is shared by many of our artists across all genres. Paul Sawyier painted watercolor impressions of Kentucky life and land; Harlan Hubbard made woodcuts and paintings that were inspired by his life in Payne Hollow and his travels on the Ohio and Mississippi Rivers. Loretta Lynn put Butcher Holler on the map for Americans who would never have heard of the place without her.

Kentucky becomes a character in the novels of modern writer Barbara Kingsolver, many of them set in the hills and forests of Appalachia. Kingsolver's fiction has blessed stacks of millions of readers since her first book, *The Bean Trees,* came out in 1988. Kingsolver spent most of her childhood in Kentucky, though her life and career has taken her to the Congo, Indiana, and Arizona. Her books, such as *The Poisonwood Bible,* hold pride of place on required reading lists (in senior year English, we were assigned *Prodigal Summer,* a transformative novel for awkward teenagers). She now makes her home in the hills of Appalachia in southern Virginia, not far from the Kentucky border. The inspiration of place can be felt in much of her writing and in many of her characters who connect with the natural solitude of the lush environments they inhabit.

Sometimes a little peace and quiet—or as quiet as those pesky cicadas will allow—is all you need to let the ideas and creative juices flow. Trappist monk Thomas Merton, who led a life of solitude at Kentucky's Abbey of Our Lady of Gethsemani, wrote more than fifty books and gained a global reputation as a social justice advocate, pacifist, and religious scholar. His enduring book *Seven Storey Mountain*, an early memoir of his journey through theology and the priesthood, inspired a generation of post–World War II seekers of peace and spiritual fulfillment. Aside from his published writings, Merton was a prolific letter writer and journal keeper as well as a frequent traveler and speaker. His thoughts were influenced by his friendships and conversations with teachers around the globe, including the Dalai Lama, Chatral Rinpoche, D. T. Suzuki, and Thich Nhat Hanh.

A devoted Catholic, Merton was one of few modern theologians to explore the relationship between Christianity and Eastern religions. Merton advocated certain Zen ideals related to the depth of the human experience and understanding one's inner life. From his hermitage at Gethsemani, Merton wrote about society and the changing nature of global politics, advocating for nonviolence and social activism. It's amazing to think that his eloquent words from the solitude of a religious order in Kentucky's central Knobs region could inspire philosophical debate in the twentieth century.

Great Kentucky Activists

Activism related to issues of the economy, equity, the environment, and social justice has often been an inspiration for Kentucky's writers. In this area, the impact of bell hooks's writing cannot be overstated. Her first book, *Ain't I a Woman: Black Women and Feminism*, changed the course of the American feminist movement, opening the door to inclusion and intersectionality.

Born Gloria Jean Watkins in Hopkinsville, hooks chose her pen name to honor her mother's mother; it is lowercased to put the emphasis on her ideas rather than her name. hooks was working on her PhD in California when *Ain't I a Woman* was released, and the world took notice. This influential intellectual and feminist icon has more than thirty books to her name, along with numerous scholarly articles, speeches, and public commentaries. bell hooks returned home to Kentucky in 2004 to a position at Berea College, where she served as Distinguished Professor in Residence in Appalachian Studies.

As with Wendell Berry, hooks felt a pull to her home place— Kentucky—as a central inspiration. Her 2008 book, *belonging: a culture of place,* included an interview with Berry. In her later career, she sought to think through and show the connection that land and land ownership has with Americans' persistent battles over race and gender equity. Her insights that "patriarchy has no gender" and that "feminism is for everybody" are rallying cries for activism and growth.

We still struggle with the effects of gender inequality and racism. Kentuckian Alice Dunnigan stated, "Race and sex were twin strikes against me. I'm not sure which was the hardest to break down."

Dunnigan was born in Russellville in western Kentucky in 1906, in a Black community that had endured the difficulties of Reconstruction and was then constrained by Jim Crow. She began writing for the newspaper in Owensboro by the time she was thirteen. Limitations on her educational and employment opportunities led her to become a teacher. Early in her teaching career, she began creating informational sheets on influential Black Kentuckians to supplement textbooks; later collected, these became *The Fascinating Story of Black Kentuckians: Their Heritage and Tradition,* a foundational historical source.

During World War II, Alice moved to Washington, DC, and began to live out her dream of being a reporter. Writing first for the *Chicago Defender* newspaper and then for the Associated Negro Press, Dunnigan interrogated the campaigns of Harry S. Truman and Dwight D. Eisenhower about the Civil Rights Movement and the struggles of Black Americans. She was the first Black female White House correspondent and the first Black female granted a Congressional press pass. These were difficult positions to be in. She was often ignored or asked to submit her questions before a press conference because President Eisenhower and his team were uncomfortable with her difficult questions about race. Her autobiography, *A Black Woman's Experience: From Schoolhouse to White House,* is a testament to her talent and resolve.

We've compiled two lists of some of our very favorite works by Kentucky writers, classic and contemporary. There's no end to good Kentucky-authored books out there. We are always adding to our reading lists, and sharing them, to promote the thoughts, beliefs, and dreams of Kentuckians.

A Classic Kentucky Reading List

Night Comes to the Cumberlands (1963)
Harry M. Caudill

The Dollmaker (1954)
Harriette Simpson Arnow

The Trail of the Lonesome Pine (1908)
John Fox Jr.

The Seven Storey Mountain (1948)
Thomas Merton

The Unsettling of America (1977)
Wendell Berry

River of Earth (1940)
James Still

All the King's Men (1946)
Robert Penn Warren

Trees of Heaven (1940)
Jesse Stuart

*Clotel; or, The President's Daughter:
A Narrative of Slave Life in the United States* (1853)
William Wells Brown

A Contemporary Kentucky Reading List

All About Love: New Visions (2000)
bell hooks

Clay's Quilt (2001)
Silas House

The Birds of Opulence (2016)
Crystal Wilkinson

The Bean Trees (1988)
Barbara Kingsolver

Horse (2023)
Geraldine Brooks

Ahab's Wife (1999)
Sena Jeter Naslund

The Sport of Kings (2016)
C. E. Morgan

The Carrying (2018)
Ada Limón

In Country (1985)
Bobbie Ann Mason

No Heroes: A Memoir of Coming Home (2002)
Chris Offut

The Mare (2015)
Mary Gaitskill

The Alphabet Mysteries (1982–2017)
Sue Grafton

Corregidora (1975)
Gayl Jones

17 | FROM MOUNTAIN MUSIC TO HIP HOP

A Kentuckian's words—written or sung, moody, joyful, or brooding—offer a powerful testament to life, love, and culture in the Bluegrass State. Our state literally invented a genre of music and also helped usher in the boy band era of the nineties. From country to jazz, hip-hop, and of course, bluegrass, Kentucky rocks. As you dive into this chapter, consider listening to this playlist while you read. As two travelers at heart, we couldn't resist throwing in one of our favorite Kentucky road-tripping soundtracks. Find "How to Rock Out Like a Kentuckian" at https://spoti.fi/3qZGVjT.

Kentucky music really started as mountain music. Early settlers didn't arrive with many musical instruments—they couldn't haul extra baggage across the Appalachian Mountains and into Kentucky. And crafting such instruments requires a lot of time, patience, and specific tools, also in short supply for these pioneers. They had to innovate.

Their desire to play music in their new home led to the creation of the mountain dulcimer, which was simpler to make than a violin. Along with the banjo and the mandolin, the dulcimer, with its sweet, plucked, resonant tones, is part of the distinctive sound of Appalachian folk music. The dulcimer is not an instrument that you'll find in many rock bands these days, but it is one of the most influential cultural objects in Appalachia. It was originally a family instrument, and songs and techniques were passed down through generations. A native of Perry County, Jean Ritchie brought the "mountain zither" to the wider world.

Ritchie, a celebrated performer and recording artist, was also a song collector. She preserved the songs that had been sung by Appalachian families since settlers first came to the hills. The youngest of fourteen children in a family of prolific singers, she benefited from the tutelage of all the "Singing Ritchies" and later notated more than three hundred songs that she had learned from her mother. Early in her career, Jean received a Fulbright scholarship and traveled to the United Kingdom, where she "swapped songs" with balladeers and folk artists and documented the Anglo and Scotch-Irish influences on the origins of mountain folk. When the American folk scene was burgeoning, Ritchie and her husband, George Pickow, had a small workshop under the Williamsburg Bridge in Brooklyn from which they sold more than three hundred dulcimers. The dulcimers were sent unfinished by her cousin Jethro Amburgey, the woodworking instructor at the Hindman Settlement School, and then were finished and tuned by George and Jean.

Bob Dylan credits Ritchie as one of his formative influences, and her songs have been covered by many artists. Johnny Cash recorded her "The L&N Don't Stop Here Anymore," and Linda Ronstadt, Dolly Parton, and Emmylou Harris all recorded her "My Dear Companion." Oh, and that bit about dulcimers not being a rock 'n' roll instrument? Cyndi Lauper, playing "Time After Time" and "True Colors" on her dulcimer, would vehemently disagree.

A dulcimer is often heard alongside other acoustic string instruments, like guitar and banjo. Add a little swing and passion from jazz and gospel music, and layer a tight "high lonesome" vocal on top, and you might just have yourself a bluegrass sound. If you've ever thought the term bluegrass music came from Kentucky's nickname, well, you'd be wrong! It came from Bill Monroe and his band, the Blue Grass Boys (but their name was chosen to honor Monroe's home state).

The Birth of Bluegrass

Monroe's career spanned nearly seventy years, and he's been inducted into the Country Music Hall of Fame, the Nashville

Songwriters Hall of Fame, and the Rock and Roll Hall of Fame. He also received a multitude of awards, including a Grammy Lifetime Achievement Award. Born in Rosine, Kentucky, in Ohio County, toward the western part of the state, Monroe's biggest influence was his uncle, "Pen" Vandiver, who was a locally famous fiddler. When Monroe and the early Blue Grass Boys won a regular spot at the Grand Ole Opry, he solidified the sound that would become bluegrass music. With his "Original Bluegrass Band," which included the legends Earl Scruggs and Lester Flatt, he wrote, performed, and recorded songs that would become classics. His most famous was a waltz, "Blue Moon of Kentucky," which became a pop hit when Elvis Presley covered it in 1954 as a B-side to "It's All Right." The tune has also been covered by Patsy Cline and Paul McCartney. Technically, McCartney has covered "Blue Moon of Kentucky" twice—a recording exists of three of the members of the Beatles playing it during an impromptu jam session. Perhaps Monroe's biggest contribution—aside from creating an entire genre of music, of course—was mentoring and helping younger musicians develop their craft. Throughout the years, the Blue Grass Boys rotated in more than 150 musicians around Bill Monroe. The Father of Bluegrass Music truly left a legacy that continues to resonate in American music.

Kentucky Country

Monroe helped usher in the American country music sound, which evolved from simple mountain tunes, to bluegrass, to cowboy and western, to the music of such country megastars as Loretta Lynn. We probably don't even have to tell you that Loretta Lynn was born a coal miner's daughter in Butcher Holler, Kentucky. With incredible achievements far too many to list—OK, we'll give it a shot: sixty albums and more than 160 songs, with ten albums at number 1 on the country music charts and sixteen singles at number 1 as well—she is the most awarded woman in country music. And while Loretta would say, "My music has no politics," it's hard not to be affected by her staunch support of working-class women and her social advocacy expressed through songs like "The Pill," "Rated X," and "Dear Uncle Sam." Her song, "You Ain't Woman Enough (To Take My Man)," was the first number 1 hit to be written by a female country artist. Her memoir, *Coal Miner's Daughter*, was turned into a hit film starring Sissy Spacek and Tommy Lee Jones. The film garnered awards and nominations—but by then Loretta had already had a star on the Hollywood Walk of Fame for three years. No big deal.

And since we've taken you all the way to Hollywood, we can't leave out two of Kentucky's most famous families: the Judds and the Clooneys. The Judds built their musical style in Ashland, in the far eastern part of the state. One of country music's most famous matriarchs, Naomi Judd, and her oldest daughter, Wynonna, rose to fame in the 1980s and became one of the most successful duos in country music history. They worked hard for their fame. In her autobiography, Naomi revealed being dismissed and even sexually harassed by producers in Nashville as she was distributing cassette tape demos. But once they got their record deal, it didn't take long to hit number 1. Their second single—1984's "Mama He's Crazy"— was the first of eight consecutive chart-toppers and won the Judds their first Grammy Award. It was the start of an incredible run of awards, in which the Judds won Best Vocal Group or Duo at both the Academy of Country Music and Country Music Association Awards from 1984 to 1990. Speaking of award winners, it'd be hard not to mention the other Judd—Naomi's younger daughter, actor Ashley, who has quite a few awards of her own. Following Naomi's diagnosis of hepatitis C in 1991, Wynonna pursued her own successful solo career. The two reunited several times for festivals and awards shows, as well as for the 1993 Super Bowl Halftime Show and a reality TV series in 2010, before Mama Judd passed away in April 2022.

About an hour and a half from Ashland headed west along the Ohio River, is Maysville, home to the famous Clooneys. In the Bluegrass State, Rosemary Clooney is often lovingly called the Maysville Matriarch. A vocal force throughout her life, she starred in films like "White Christmas" and recorded a slew of hit songs and albums, one of which included "Pennies from Heaven." That well-known tune inspires visitors to leave pennies on her headstone in the Maysville cemetery, something that never fails to make us smile. Rosemary's brother, Nick, is a successful journalist, anchorman, and television host. We imagine the brother–sister duo was an inspiration to their nephew/son, George, who was also born in Kentucky but left to pursue a career in Hollywood. You may have heard of him; pretty sure he has a star on the Hollywood Walk of Fame, too.

Jazz and Hip-Hop

In addition to music stars with big-name recognition, Kentucky is also home to a less well-known musical legacy. Among the earliest Kentucky settlers were slaves and free Black people who brought their own cultural influences to the music of the region. African American spirituals, work songs, blues, and later, jazz permeated Kentucky. You can hear the influence in Jean Ritchie's swapped folk songs through to Nappy Roots's unique Kentucky hip-hop. At the turn of the twentieth century, Louisville was particularly rich with Jazz Age musicians developing a smooth new sound.

Edith Wilson is an all-too-often-forgotten titan of the Jazz Age. Born in Louisville toward the end of the nineteenth century—*she'd* tell you it was 1906, but only because she wanted folks to think she was ten years younger than she actually was—Wilson dominated vaudeville, clubs, and theater stages. Wilson was a classic cabaret blues singer who brought in crowds from Louisville to Harlem to London. She didn't record many albums during her career, but she performed with other megastars of the time, like Fletcher Henderson, Florence Mills, Louis Armstrong, Fats Waller, and Cab Calloway. Later in her career, Wilson acted in radio, television, and film, leading to her best-remembered role as the face of Aunt Jemima. From 1948 to 1966, Edith Wilson portrayed the stereotypical "mammy" figure for the Quaker Oats brand in print and broadcast advertisements, as well as in public appearances. By the time of the Civil Rights Act of 1964 and the Voting Rights Act of 1965, Wilson's role as Aunt Jemima was getting lots of heat from the NAACP and the Black community for its problematic racial stereotyping, leading Quaker Oats to phase out her public portrayals. Before her death in 1981, Wilson performed one final time at the Newport Folk Festival in 1980.

Hip-hop, like jazz, is an important cultural touchstone for Black artists. Kentucky wasn't usually mentioned in the southern hip-hop conversation, until the aughts brought the album "Watermelon, Chicken & Gritz" from Nappy Roots. Fish Scales (born in Tennessee, but we'll forgive him), Skinny DeVille, B. Stille, Ron Clutch, Big V, and R. Prophet met as students at Western Kentucky University in Bowling Green. Their eclectic, alternative style of rap-rock was a hit in the mainstream. For many of us who were teenagers in the early 2000s, Nappy Roots's first single, "Awnaw," was a must-have on every playlist. The top-selling hip-hop artists of 2002 followed their debut with six more albums, and more hits, including "Good Day." One of the first of its kind, but definitely not the last, Nappy Roots ushered in Kentucky's own roster of southern hip-hop lyricists, including Bryson Tiller, Jack Harlow, and EST Gee.

The continued legacy of Kentucky music is one of a patchwork of styles and experiences, born of the sounds of the cities, mountains, and farms. The Kentucky sound can be experienced via plucked strings on porches, on stage, on a turntable, and even using streaming. You can explore the legacy at Renfro Valley in Rockcastle County, the Kentucky Opry in Draffenville, the Bluegrass Music Hall of Fame & Museum in Owensboro, and the Mountain Arts Center in Prestonsburg. You can visit a McDonald's full of Everly Brothers memorabilia in their hometown of Central City or put pennies on Rosemary Clooney's gravesite in Maysville. The Kentucky sound echoes.

18 | FAMOUS MINDS WITH FAMOUS IDEAS

Kentucky has been a powerhouse of new ideas from the start. The challenges of living and thriving in the varied geographic areas of Kentucky fostered inventiveness and creativity among its inhabitants, from the earliest native Americans who farmed and hunted the land, to the European explorers who first entered the region in the late 1600s and then settled there. As pioneers trailblazed through the Cumberland Gap in the wake of Daniel Boone, they faced numerous difficulties in the unfamiliar territory. As they carved out a new life, they developed new tools to meet new needs.

The genius born of necessity is a proud legacy in our state. Early achievements led to breakthroughs in education, science, business, the arts, and medicine. With this heritage, Kentuckians have been inspired to continue to innovate and modernize. And today, they are credited with a slew of unique, ingenious inventions, many of which are used across the world.

Knives, Bats, and Patents

What better way to carve out a new life than with a really good knife? The Bowie knife has become famous as a distinctively American weapon, particularly after its namesake, James Bowie, wielded a version at the Alamo during the Texas Revolution. But the origins of the knife are arguable. We'll give you the Kentucky version. James, or "Jim," Bowie—who was born in Logan County, Kentucky—loved to carry a long hunting knife. Following an infamous altercation known as the Sandbar Fight, Jim was gifted a new style of knife by his brother, Rezin. But it's the maker of Rezin's gift that has been debated over the past century and a half. Rezin claimed he designed the blade, while his grandchildren insisted that he only ever supervised his blacksmith, who was the actual designer. What did Jim Bowie, who made the knife famous, say? He said it was Kentucky blacksmith Lovell Snowden who designed and forged the weapon. Regardless, we can definitely correct one common error—the knife's name is pronounced *Boo-ee.*

The Commonwealth hits it out of the park with another, perhaps its best-known, invention—the Louisville Slugger. It's a story that really ought to be a movie. Picture it: a young son, helping his father in his woodworking shop, sneaks away to a local baseball game where one of his sports heroes breaks his bat in another frustrating attempt during a hitting slump. The boy invites the player back to the shop and offers to make a new bat with better specifications. And, bam! In his next at bat, the sports star nails three hits with his new signature equipment. According to the history of the Hillerich family, original manufacturers of the bat, it's entirely true! The son of a German immigrant who opened his shop in Louisville in 1855, John "Bud" Hillerich made the first bat for Louisville Eclipse star Pete Browning in 1884. Pete's nickname? The Louisville Slugger. Since then, the Louisville Slugger has been the bat of choice for nearly every Major League Baseball player and every playing level below the pros. In 1905, Pittsburgh Pirates star Honus Wagner became the first professional athlete to sign a paid endorsement deal with Louisville Slugger, and Americans got to know the brand as they watched their favorite players like Babe Ruth, Ty Cobb, and Lou Gehrig swing for the fences. Today, Louisville hosts an MLB AAA team, the Louisville Bats—named in honor of the signature Kentucky product.

It only makes sense that one of Kentucky's most visionary leaders would also be a great inventor. Abraham Lincoln, a Kentucky son no matter what Illinois claims, is the only US president to have registered a patent. Lincoln's design of a device to lift a boat over shoals or obstructions in a river was inspired by his experiences as a teen riding on a flatboat down the Ohio and Mississippi Rivers. This invention, never manufactured, relied on a system of water-proof fabric bladders along the base of the boat. The bladders could be inflated to lift the boat to the surface of the water, allowing it to clear an obstacle. During his presidency, Lincoln spoke in favor of patents several times, noting that the system benefited both the inventor and society.

Kentuckians are known for having thought up a number of other notable things, some of them familiar parts of everyday life. For example, every time you sing "Happy Birthday to You," you owe it to two Kentucky sisters, Mildred and Patty Hill, who created and published the tune. And Kentuckians invented the stoplight, the high five, and the Tommy gun. Some Kentucky contributions that have left their mark on the world have been the products of researchers at state-of-the-art institutions of higher education. Then again, those Happy Birthday sisters were kindergarten teachers, so maybe the genius takes root in our earliest years around here.

Educating Great Minds

We can't talk about the great minds of Kentucky without talking about our great institutions of higher education. The state benefited from the traditions of universities established earlier in Virginia and the northeastern United States, but Transylvania was the first university west of the Allegheny Mountains. Transy, as the locals call it, was not named for Dracula's legendary birthplace; the name comes from Latin and means "across the woods," a tribute to Kentucky's lush, green environment. Transylvania began as a seminary in a log cabin in Boyle County, and, in 1789, it moved to Gratz Park in Lexington, where it still stands today. Famously, following the establishment of the university, Thomas Jefferson proclaimed Lexington the "Athens of the West."

At Transylvania University, Constantine Samuel Rafinesque became renowned as a naturalist and educator. His impressive name seems to fit with the rather spooky one of the university. In fact, Transy's mascot, a bat, is named "Raf" in his honor. More accurately, it's named after the bat species to which he also lent his name: *Corynorhinus rafinesquii,* Rafinesque's big-eared bat. Rafinesque was a self-trained autodidact and polymath—come again? Translation: He was self-taught and knew about a lot of things. These days, he'd be your Phone-A-Friend call. Rafinesque collected his extensive knowledge from wide-ranging reading and the many expeditions he made in Europe and the Ottoman Empire before he moved permanently to the United States.

Rafinesque applied to join the Lewis and Clark Expedition twice but was rejected by Thomas Jefferson both times. A regrettable decision, perhaps. He became one of the first naturalists to use the word "evolution," and even wrote on the phenomenon while Darwin was still cruising aboard the *Beagle* and drawing finches. As he explored the United States, rebuilding his specimen collection, Rafinesque made his first trip to Kentucky, where he stayed for several weeks at John James Audubon's home in Henderson County. The following year, he landed at Transylvania University as a professor of botany, where he cultivated his eccentric reputation. Although he left the university after a quarrel with the president in 1826, you can actually visit him at the college today. His body was reinterred at Transy in 1924 (he passed in 1840), in a tomb inscribed "Honor to whom honor is overdue."

Allegedly, upon Rafinesque's contentious departure, he cursed the president and the college—the curse is said to recur every seven years. To stave off bad luck and ill happenings, Transylvania students now appease Rafinesque's spirit and honor his time at Transy by keeping vigil in his tomb on Halloween night.

Education in Kentucky—particularly higher education—has historically been rather progressive. By establishing schools and social programs to fit specific needs, Kentuckians have always found a way to help one another and to better their home state.

Berea College, southeast of Lexington, is one such cherished Kentucky institution. The first college in the American South to be both racially integrated and coeducational, Berea was established in 1855 by abolitionist minister John Gregg Fee. Today, as then, Berea charges no tuition fees whatsoever. The school offers comprehensive work-study programs that aid students financially and also serve the needs of the school and community. Berea is consistently ranked in the top tier of liberal arts and regional universities, and, as they jokingly note on their website, they offer "the best education money can't buy."

The Mark of Kentucky Women

We are proud to teach people about the incredible impact of women throughout Kentucky's history. One example would be Madeline McDowell Breckinridge, a member of a privileged family with a tradition of philanthropy and activism that pulled frontier Kentucky into the modern era. During the nineteenth and twentieth centuries, Madeline exemplified the Kentucky ideal. A great-granddaughter of famed Kentucky statesman Henry Clay, she grew up at the Ashland estate in Lexington. Madeline was a great-niece of Dr. Ephraim McDowell, renowned surgeon and namesake of the hospital in Danville, and a cousin of Laura Clay, who founded the Kentucky Equal Rights Association. Through her marriage to Desha Breckinridge—the editor of the *Lexington Herald*—she was also the sister-in-law of Sophonisba Breckinridge, a Progressive activist and the first woman to pass the Kentucky bar exam.

From an impressive family, Madeline herself fills volumes with her accomplishments. While her deep privilege and inherited wealth gave her public prominence, she used her platform and connections to zealously advocate for progressive social reforms. Advocating child labor laws and compulsory school attendance, and founding programs for poverty relief and for public health care for tuberculosis patients, Madeline McDowell Breckinridge worked tirelessly both locally and nationally. She was her most vocal when speaking for the Women's Suffrage Movement. She and her husband used the editorial pages of his newspaper to help turn the tide of public opinion, and Madeline herself served as president of the Kentucky Equal Rights Association and vice president of the National American Woman Suffrage Association. She passed away on November 25, 1920, just twenty-three days after she had voted in the 1920 presidential election, the first election following Kentucky's ratification of the Nineteenth Amendment.

Another notable woman in Kentucky history, Mary Carson Breckinridge, established the Frontier Nursing Service in 1925. In the early twentieth century, much of the United States was still considered the frontier. Few public utilities and even fewer medical or dental services were available in the Appalachian Mountains of Eastern Kentucky, and Mary Breckinridge was witness to the struggle of women and children in her community to survive without their basic healthcare needs met.

Deploying trained nurse-midwives on horseback, the FNS served an area of more than seven hundred miles with prenatal, midwifery, and family health assistance. Along with their saddlebags packed with medical supplies, the nurse-midwives brought newfangled notions of germ theory and sanitation; they improved infection and birth rates as well as health outcomes for a vast population. In 1939, the Frontier Nursing Service established a formal graduate program to educate and train nurse-midwives who would practice in their rural communities. Nearly one hundred years later, Frontier Nursing University in Versailles continues to graduate health practitioners and now operates clinical centers not just in Kentucky, but nationwide. Its graduates gain practical knowledge and serve the community.

Well-Deserved Recognition

As of 2020, the Nobel Prize has been awarded 603 times to 962 individuals, two of them Kentuckians. Both were geneticists: Thomas Hunt Morgan received the award in 1933 and Phillip A. Sharp in 1993. Morgan's work with flies demonstrated how chromosomes pass on hereditary traits, and Sharp worked with RNA and discovered split genes. They both received their undergraduate degrees from Kentucky universities—Morgan got a BS from State College (now the University of Kentucky) and Sharp a BA in chemistry and mathematics from Union College in Barbourville. Morgan, a founding father of genetics, is particularly known for expanding and codifying many of Gregor Mendel's theories of heredity. Morgan crossbred fruit flies (*Drosophila melanogaster*) to study inheritance patterns in mutations of eye color. His lab's success with the use of fruit flies led the species to become one of the most widely used model organisms in genetic experiments. Dr. Sharp himself has collaborated on two papers that use *Drosophila melanogaster* as their research subject. Could some lingering influence from the roving naturalist Rafinesque have been an inspiration for Morgan and Sharp's fly collecting years later?

Kentucky Bucket List

There's a lot of fun to be had in Kentucky. We have great traditions of food, drink, and celebrations, and undeniably, a certain special (even sometimes peculiar) way of doing and saying things. But we're here and who we are today because of those who came before us, people of great creativity, intellect, and talent. We love to share about their contributions to our home state. Here are a few items to add to that Kentucky Bucket list that will give you more insight into the Commonwealth's great thinkers.

1. Take a trip to the Frazier Kentucky History Museum in Louisville. At the Frazier Kentucky History Museum, exhibits and live performances examine history, bourbon, music, arts, and culture to showcase the achievements of Kentuckians. See the boat Tori Murden McClure rowed solo across the Atlantic Ocean—the first woman and the first American to do so. Learn the story of Cabbage Patch Kids, invented by Kentuckian Martha Nelson Thomas (we had a few hundred of those dolls growing up!). Hear about how architect John A. Roebling, designer of the Brooklyn Bridge, had first built a similar bridge that connected Covington, Kentucky, to Cincinnati, Ohio. And find out more about that patent of Abraham Lincoln's we mentioned earlier.

2. Rock out at the Kentucky Music Hall of Fame in Renfro Valley. This museum and hall of fame opened in 2002 to bring recognition to Kentuckians who have made a significant contribution to the music industry. Its collection of artifacts and memorabilia that highlight the careers of more than fifty inductees, including Loretta Lynn, Florence Henderson, Rosemary Clooney, Boots Randolph, and the Backstreet Boys, will appeal to a wide range of tastes.

3. Pick up a book by a Kentucky author at your local library or small bookstore. Wendell Berry, Hunter S. Thompson, bell hooks, Saeed Jones, Sue Grafton, our list could go on and on. There are so many immensely talented Kentucky writers and incredible works to choose from. Start with Bobbie Ann Mason or Barbara Kingsolver—you won't regret it.

4. Visit a historic home or monument around the state. From Henry Clay and Thomas Hunt Morgan to Thomas Edison and Abraham Lincoln (oh, and Mary Todd Lincoln, too!), there are so many great historic homes and monuments to visit across Kentucky. Learn about the Commonwealth's rich history and traditions, its profound statesmen, how we've grown and learned from generations before us, and how that history has shaped the Kentucky we know today.

5. Discover Shaker Village at Pleasant Hill. This village in the heart of Central Kentucky, once home to the Pleasant Hill community of Shakers, has three thousand acres of beautiful farmland and thirty-four restored nineteenth-century buildings. During the group's 105-year span, the Shakers used skilled craftsmanship to build a community with iconic architecture. But even more interesting is the history of this religious group, how they ended up in Kentucky, and why they eventually became, for lack of a better phrase, extinct. Learn more about these craftsmen and women who were using methods and tools far ahead of their time.

Suggested Reading

We built you a great beginning reading list a few pages ago and gave you a playlist to enjoy, but we know there is so much more to be learned from the state's most prolific writers, inventors, thinkers, singers, and artists. We suggest you start with learning a bit more from a few of these great venues and works.

Websites

Bluegrass Music Hall of Fame and Museum, Owensboro. https://www.bluegrasshall.org/.

Kentucky Artisan Center at Berea. https://kentuckyartisan center.ky.gov/.

Kentucky Center for African American Heritage, Louisville. https://kcaah.org/.

Kentucky Folk Art Center, Morehead. https://www.morehead state.edu/outreach/kentucky-folk-art-center.

Kentucky Main Streets Program. https://www.kentuckytourism .com/culture/kentucky-main-streets.

Kentucky Music Hall of Fame. https://www.kentuckymusichall offame.com/.

KMAC Museum, Louisville. https://www.kmacmuseum.org/.

Mountain Arts Center, Prestonsburg. https://macarts.com/.

Renfro Valley Entertainment Center, Mount Vernon. https:// renfrovalley.com/.

Roots 101 African-American Museum. https://www.roots-101 .org/.

Speed Art Museum, Louisville. https://www.speedmuseum.org/.

University of Kentucky Art Museum. https://finearts.uky.edu /art-museum.

US 23 Country Music Highway Museum, Staffordsville. http:// paintsvilletourism.com/index.php/attractions/.

Books

Clark, Jerry E. *The Shawnee*. Lexington: University Press of Kentucky, 2007.

Hall, Wade, ed. *The Kentucky Anthology: Two Hundred Years of Writing in the Bluegrass.* Lexington: University Press of Kentucky, 2005.

Hay, Melba Porter. *Madeline McDowell Breckinridge and the Battle for a New South.* Lexington: University Press of Kentucky, 2009.

Irvin, Helen D. *Women in Kentucky.* Lexington: University Press of Kentucky, 2009.

Kleber, John E., ed. *The Kentucky Encyclopedia.* Lexington: University Press of Kentucky, 1992.

Klotter, James C., and Freda C. *A Concise History of Kentucky.* Lexington: University Press of Kentucky, 2008.

———. *Faces of Kentucky.* Lexington: University Press of Kentucky, 2006.

Ritchie, Jean. *Singing Family of the Cumberlands.* Lexington: University Press of Kentucky, 1988.

Stuart, Jesse. *Kentucky Is My Land.* Ashland: Jesse Stuart Foundation, 1988.

Worley, Jeff. *What Comes Down to Us: 25 Contemporary Kentucky Poets.* Lexington: University Press of Kentucky, 2009.

ACKNOWLEDGMENTS

I never met a Kentuckian who wasn't either thinking
about going home or actually going home.

ALBERT B. "HAPPY" CHANDLER

A book always seems like a wonderful idea,
but books are also the sort of
things where you forget about the
blood, sweat, and tears shortly
after you finish and then sud-
denly remember all of that in
vivid detail the moment you sit down to do it all over again. This
particular book is our first off-road My Old Kentucky Road Trip,
and thus, it was a unique kind of adventure for these two longtime
friends and writing partners.

In many ways, we've gotten used to living in separate states
after having lived only moments away from each other for most of
our lives. In many ways, we've mastered the phone call/video call/
text message/email communication that helps us stay connected
as friends and as authors. But projects like this one help keep us
anchored together and to Kentucky. We say it after every book—I
don't think we can do that again! But somehow, we always do, and
we're always hungry for another one.

Thanks to Patrick O'Dowd, Margaret Kelly, Ashley Runyon,
Jackie Wilson, David Cobb, the editorial, production, design, and
marketing teams, and the whole of the fantastic University Press
of Kentucky for giving us this opportunity to do what we said we

couldn't do. It is a privilege to work with this Kentucky-based publisher for the first time as authors and with Ashley again.

To our dear friend and agent, Alice Speilburg at Speilburg Literary Agency—thank you for continuing to stick with us against what is probably your much better judgment. You make the tough parts look easy and the process smooth and seamless so we can focus on what we do best: procrastinating. We absolutely would not survive a book without your guidance and advice.

Additionally, we are so thankful to have connected with the immensely talented illustrator Jessica Rusher for this project. Jessica, your beautiful illustrations are everything we didn't know this book needed. Thank you for bringing our mini Kentucky visions to life.

While Elliott Hess didn't provide images for this book, he continues to supply us with breathtaking photographs of our favorite Kentucky places and moments for our social media accounts. We remain grateful for you.

Thanks to our littlest roadtripper, Louie, who is always up for an adventure. And thank you to our Troop who have always supported and encouraged us on this and many other journeys, and who are always there with a laugh.

We owe so much to our families, who not only endlessly support us, but whose own Kentucky roots planted ours. We are forever grateful for your stories—they inspire our own.

And finally, we can't write a book about the history, traditions, and culture of Kentucky without acknowledging those who came before all of us and the history we're still learning from today.

ACKNOWLEDGING OUR PRESENCE ON INDIGENOUS LAND

Indigenous peoples have always lived on the land that is now called Kentucky, and they continue to live here today. The place we now call Kentucky encompasses primarily Shawnee, Cherokee, Chickasaw, and Osage land; however, other tribes, including the Miami and Quapaw, also called this place home.

Indigenous peoples have lived on this land for at least twelve thousand years. They did not just use the land as a hunting ground—that myth was first propagated by land speculators and is still repeated today as a way to absolve the Commonwealth's settlers and their descendants from their history of land theft and genocide. The land was a home to various indigenous nations and cultures.

Over the years, these indigenous nations have helped shape the Kentucky we know today. Those who have avoided or survived forced relocation efforts over the past few hundred years have not done so without effort. Thousands of indigenous people still call the Commonwealth home but have been forced to keep their languages and traditions quiet. Their collective history and culture is vast, and it is the responsibility of other Kentuckians today to learn carefully and respectfully.

INDEX

ABOUT THE AUTHORS

Blair Thomas Hess is a born-and-bred Kentuckian who grew up traveling and learning about the state with her family. Today she works to promote the Commonwealth's culture and traditions in order to teach others about her home state. She lives in Frankfort with her daughter and husband.

Cameron M. Ludwick calls Kentucky her birthplace and Lexington her hometown. Though she now lives in Austin, Texas, she never misses an opportunity to remind Lone Star State residents that everything good came from Kentucky first.

Together, these longtime friends are the authors of four travel books about Kentucky, including *My Old Kentucky Road Trip* and *The State of Bourbon*. You can follow their travel journeys at myoldkentuckyroadtrip.com or on Instagram @myoldkyroadtrip.